LIVE LOVED

Growing into Jesus' *Love*

TY SALTZGIVER

LUCIDBOOKS

Live Loved: Growing Into Jesus' Love

Published by Lucid Books in Houston, TX
www.LucidBooks.com

ISBN: 978-1-63296-979-8
eISBN: 978-1-63296-980-4

Special Sales: Most Lucid Books titles are available in special quantity discounts. Custom imprinting or excerpting can also be done to fit special needs. Contact Lucid Books at Info@LucidBooks.com

TABLE OF CONTENTS

WHY THIS BOOK?

Jesus loves me! We know that. But do our jaws drop in sheer awe when we hear that sentence… that reality?

Yes, we believe "Jesus loves me." That's Christianity 101. Now we say, "Let's move on to a higher-level class." No, that is the highest level we can take. In fact, "Jesus loves me" is the name of the degree of Christianity. The thesis of our doctoral work for our PhD in the field of "Growing as a Christian" is, "Jesus loves me."

Why then, when we teach how to grow closer to Jesus through discipleship today, does it seem to focus mostly on gaining more knowledge and improving our behavior? This book moves "Jesus loves me" back to its rightful place as the most essential part of our friendship with Jesus.

* * * * *

Most of us would nod our heads, "Yes," in answering the question: "Do you believe Jesus loves you?" But how many of us would go on and say that the biggest impact on our daily lives, the biggest thing that shapes our identity, has been and is currently: Jesus' love for us? The percentage answering yes to that question is much smaller. Why is that?

Do we believe Jesus loves us in our heads, but His love hasn't captured our hearts? Romans 10:9 uses the phrase, "believe in your heart" to describe this. Does our knowing we are not worthy of His love keep us from receiving Jesus' love in our deepest place, our innermost being (even unconsciously)? Has the "bad" that has happened in our lives, and the horrible things we see happening in the world, left us questioning or doubting Jesus' love? Do we think Jesus' love is great, but there's more we need to have the full life we desire?

* * * * *

The apostle John refers to himself five times in his Gospel as "the disciple whom Jesus loves" (John 13:23; 19:26; 20:2; 21:7; 21:20). He wasn't being arrogant, nor claiming a special status compared to the other disciples. That's just how he knew himself, saw himself, and defined himself.

Let's say you have a new friendship you're really excited about. He/she asks you, "Tell me a little about yourself." You feel safe, so you are not measuring your words. You begin to share a bit of your life story. Would you include, "I am the disciple whom Jesus loves"? Probably not. Why is that?

Is it because you've never thought that way of yourself? Or if you did think that way, do you think that would be a designation for the really super committed Christian but not for you?

The Greek word we translate as *disciple* is *mathetes.* It means "learner" or "student." When you accepted Jesus and committed to living your life in a friendship with Him, you became a *mathetes*, a disciple, of Jesus. You've already said that you would answer "yes" to the question: "Do you believe Jesus loves you?" Therefore, you are "the disciple whom Jesus loves." What would it take for you to see yourself with that designation?

* * * * *

When we talk about discipleship, or growing spiritually, what is it we primarily talk about? Is it Bible study, gaining more knowledge, and getting our doctrines correct? Is it aligning our lives with Jesus' teaching and living according to Christian values? Is it growing into the image of Jesus (Romans 8:29; 2 Corinthians 3:18)? Is it fulfilling the Great Commission by sharing Jesus with others (Matthew 28:19)? Or is it finding our place to serve in ministry, using the gifts Jesus has given us?

Of course, all those are right and good. But why is the transformation of our hearts not at the top of our list of what constitutes discipleship? Shouldn't there be more focus on our hearts?

Is there any spiritual growth apart from knowing Jesus' love more deeply in our hearts? (After all, God is actually Love – 1 John 4:8.) "Jesus loves me" is not just the beginning point of spiritual growth, nor just the foundation, nor just the scaffolding of spiritual growth; rather it is everything.

Our heart is the control center of our entire self. Doesn't everything spring from our hearts? Proverbs 4:23 says, "Guard your heart above all else, for it determines the course of your life" (NLT).

Listen to Jesus:

> Each tree is known by its fruit. You don't get good fruit from a bad tree, nor do you get bad fruit from a good tree… You don't pick figs from a thorn bush, nor pick grapes from a briar bush. A good person brings forth what is good out of the good stored up in his heart, and an evil person brings forth what is evil from the evil stored up in his heart. For the mouth speaks and the body acts from that which fills the heart. (Luke 6:43-46, my personal translation)

He also says in Mark 7:

> Nothing that enters a person from the outside can defile a person. For it doesn't go into

> the heart but into the stomach and then is eliminated out of the body… What comes out of a person is what can defile them. For it is from within, out of a person's heart, that evil thoughts and actions come: sexual immorality, hate, greed, malice, deceit, envy, slander, arrogance and folly. All these come from the heart… (verses 18-23, my personal translation)

You know what transforms a heart? Love does. Being loved does. Receiving Jesus' love into our hearts does. Discipleship should include not just believing Jesus loves us but also experiencing Jesus' love. Discipleship should include more learning to let Jesus love us, more of our growing into Jesus' love, and knowing our belovedness in Him.

There is a huge difference between an intellectual knowing of Jesus' love, or a cognitive knowing of Jesus' love, and of Jesus' love capturing your heart and empowering your life.

* * * * *

Dallas Willard says in *The Divine Conspiracy*, "It is confidence in the invariably overriding intention of God for our good, even with respect to all the evil and suffering that may befall us on life's journey, that secures us peace and joy."[2]

I would add that knowing in your innermost being that Jesus loves you above all your life choices for good or bad, and above all your own personal suffering, just or unjust, is what leads to freedom and purpose and excitement for living and empowerment in being who you are meant to be. You and I are made to be filled with the love of Jesus.

A WORD BEFORE

Three thoughts as we begin:

1. So many of us learn the facts, a propositional Christianity. We learn that Jesus loves us as a truth, a doctrine to adopt as a Christian. What happens then is we completely lose the reality that Christianity is, first and foremost, a love story. And we are in it. We are the ones loved. Loved by God. Loved by Jesus. We desire to draw closer to Jesus. Learning to let Jesus love us is a vital part of drawing closer to Him.
2. I wish knowing Jesus' love for us would be a "check the box." Now, what is next? Here's the reality: When you accepted Jesus and committed your life to Him, asked Him to come live in your heart, and received Jesus' love for you, you became His beloved child (John 1:12). However, from that moment on, you are also on the journey of growing into Jesus' love for you. This is a true statement: I am the beloved

of Jesus, and I am still growing into my belovedness. As Henri Nouwen stated: "Becoming the Beloved is the great spiritual journey we have to make."[3]

Jesus' love for us can be compared to love in a marriage. When I came down the aisle after our wedding service, I looked at Ann and said, "I love you, Ann," and I meant it with all my being. Ann and I have now been married forty-four years, and last night Ann went to bed a little earlier than I did because I was watching basketball. I kissed Ann good night and said, "I love you, Ann." I meant it with all my being. That love, however, had grown to be a deeper, richer, wider love than the love of our wedding day. It grew over time and through our doing life together. Ann's knowing of my love for her has also grown to be deeper, richer, and wider. She has grown more confident and secure in my love for her. She no longer guards her heart from opening and even surrenders to my love for her. She knows more deeply that she is cherished and adored. She sees herself easily as my beloved.

That is what it's like to grow into Jesus' love. The example breaks down in that Jesus' love for us doesn't actually grow, because it is already infinite love, omni-love, perfect love. It's just our understanding, knowing, and receiving His Love into our innermost place that grows more deeply over time.

3. Not only did Jesus create each one of us uniquely and wonderfully in His very Image, but He also reveals Himself to each of us in a unique way, particular to us. And He grows each of us uniquely based on our personalities, families, culture of origin, life experiences, our own wounding and wiring, etc.

To undertake writing from my uniqueness, and the uniqueness of Jesus growing me, that would apply to your uniqueness, and the uniqueness of Jesus growing you, is quite a challenge. This book certainly represents my fifty-six years of living life in a friendship with Jesus. You might even title my own story: One Who is Growing into Jesus' Love. What we have in common, though, is that Jesus loves us and wants each of us to know His love in our deepest place. He wants our belovedness in Him to be the foundation of our relationship with Him and of our lives. We can truly live loved!

CHAPTER 1

You can take all I've ever taught or written and sum it up with: Jesus loves me, this I know.
—Karl Barth, the great Swiss theologian

We sang the lyrics, "Jesus loves me, this I know, for the Bible tells me so," as kids. And we believed it then. But as adults living in an alien world, precious little sings of Jesus' love. Our culture, with its value system, the barrage of messages from the TV, advertisements, movies and music, all woo us away from Jesus and makes His love irrelevant. Our phones and screen time constantly distract us, satan bombards us with his lies and seduction, and we build our identities around things of this world. We know we are not worthy, and unexpected suffering and pain have us doubting God's good intention toward us, as well as His Love for us. Our busyness holds us captive, and we all have unanswered prayers. All of this makes us wonder what knowing "Jesus loves me" even means for our everyday lives.

I wish that when you read these next few sentences, you will be overwhelmed, even brought to tears.

Jesus loves you! Jesus loves you "without caution, limit, boundary or breaking point."[4] Jesus' love for you has nothing to do with you; it is regardless of you. The Inventor of love, Jesus, chooses to bestow His love on the object of His love…that's you…and that's me. There is no mistake, failure, wrong, brokenness, wound, evil thought, or despicable act you've committed that disqualifies you from the full extent of Jesus' love for you. You cannot earn His love, nor diminish His love for you by any good deed or by any errant deed. It's yours, given to you.

Remember Jesus' parable about the Extravagant Father (Luke 15:11-32). (I know we refer to that parable as The Prodigal Son, but it is wrongly named. It's all about the Extravagant Father's love for his two sons, both of whom didn't recognize it, nor receive it.)

You know the story. If you were asked the question, "When did the father love the wayward son the most?" Most answer quickly, "Why of course, when he returned home. The father kissed him incessantly, put the family signet ring on his finger, dressed him in a clean robe, gave him sandals, and threw him a party." Yes, the father certainly loved his son then.

But on deeper thinking, did the father love his son when he gave him half of his estate knowing he was going to leave and probably blow it all? How does the old saying go? If you love something, you let it go. If it comes back to you, it's yours forever. If it doesn't come back, then it was never yours.

In *Beauty and the Beast*, Belle sees her father in the magic mirror. And he is in big trouble. She asks the beast if she can go to him. The beast says, "Yes, you must go," knowing fully that the last rose petal will fall from the rose and he'll be a beast forever, according to the curse. Completely dumbfounded, the clock and the candlestick ask the beast, "How could you let her go?" The beast responds, "Because I love her." Love never enslaves.

The father loved his son greatly when he let him go. His heartache tells him so.

Didn't the father love his son as he would stand on his porch, day after day (for years?), searching the horizon for his son's figure to appear on the horizon… for his coming home?

In other words, there wasn't a moment in his son's life that the father didn't love his son. He never loved him any less or any more.

There's never been a moment in your life that you haven't been loved by Jesus to the full extent of His love. Jesus loved you as He dreamed you up, as He knit you together in your mother's womb, as He birthed you, and as He has watched over you every moment of every day of your life. And He can't wait to love you for eternity, even when you pass from this earth.

In Psalm 103, David describes the greatness of God's love for us in this way, "As high as the heavens are above the earth, so great is His lovingkindness toward those who revere me" (verse 11). Then he goes on to say, "God's love for you is from everlasting to everlasting for those who revere him" (verse 17a).

Jesus wants you and me to know His Love. His love is not like the rabbit out in front of the greyhounds that they can never catch. Jesus wants us to catch His love. He's not holding back, waiting to see if we meet certain criteria.

Moving beyond "Jesus loves me" as a propositional truth to really experiencing Jesus' love is both a challenge and a necessity in our lives. We easily accept ideas and beliefs about Jesus but have no personal experience of Him. Once you experience Jesus' love, nothing else compares. You desire to grow into His love more than anything else on earth.

Jonathan Edwards used the analogy of "knowing about honey" versus "tasting honey" for yourself. You can study honey and understand its origin and learn that it is sweet to the taste. Other respected friends can tell you that honey, in fact, tastes sweet. You can come to actually believe that honey is sweet. But until you taste it, you don't truly know its sweetness. The excellency and sweetness of honey is in its taste, Edwards argues, therefore the person who loves honey because of its taste builds upon the foundation of honey's sweetness. If you don't know the taste of honey, you can't truly know honey's sweetness.[5]

Edward's analogy applies to Jesus' love for you. Do you just know *about* Jesus' love for you, or have you *experienced* His love for you, having tasted it for yourself? Or, said a different way: when Mary, the mother of Jesus, saw and heard the shepherd's vision of the angels and the heavenly host rejoicing, she "treasured up all these things and pondered them in her heart" (Luke 2:19 NIV). Meaning, it wasn't just a seeing and understanding of these things, she took them inside herself, letting them have an effect in her deepest place.

When you think about what it is that Jesus wants from you, what comes to mind? Does Jesus primarily want your worship? Your obedience? Your service? Your belief?

Jesus primarily wants a love relationship with you. Jesus longs to love you. He wants you to know you are loved. In fact, that's what you were made for: to be filled with His love. That's what makes you come alive. His love makes you fully satisfied, experiencing freedom, peace, and joy. Jesus wants us to live loved.

Brennan Manning said this about knowing Jesus' love for you, "Maybe you know about Jesus' love, but you haven't believed it for yourself; or, you've believed it, but you haven't accepted it; or, you've accepted it, but you haven't surrendered to it."[6] When you think about growing into Jesus' love for you, does that statement ring true?

I might amend Manning's statement to read: "Maybe you know about Jesus' love, but you haven't believed it for yourself; or, you've believed it, but haven't accepted it; or, you've accepted it, but you've never really tasted Jesus' love, never experienced it, never received Jesus' love into your deepest place."

How can we grow more into Jesus' love for us? How can we taste it more deeply? How can we grow into knowing His great love for us and know ourselves as His beloved sons/daughters?

Everything in our relationship with God is His Grace given to us. St. Augustine clearly teaches that even the desire to turn to God, that too is a gift from God.[7] The scales falling from your eyes for you to really see Jesus, and the crust breaking from around your heart for you to be able to desire and accept Jesus, is grace at work. Jesus said, "No one can come to Me unless the Father who sent Me draws him..." (John 6:44). The apostle Paul said, "For by grace you have been saved through faith; and this is not of yourselves, it is the gift of God; not a result of works, so that no one may boast" (Ephesians 2:8-9).

Therefore, experiencing in your deepest place that Jesus loves you is a gift of God; it is Grace. To grow into Jesus' love is embedded in, and empowered by, His Grace. Knowing yourself as the disciple whom Jesus loves is a movement of the Holy Spirit and Jesus from within our hearts.

Exercise #1

Begin asking God to help you grow into Jesus' love for you. You probably haven't prayed that prayer (or at least not as a daily prayer). You can pray in your own words, something like, "Please Jesus, help me grow into Your love, into my belovedness in you." Keep it simple like that. Or, "Help me receive Your love into my innermost being." Or maybe pray a version of Psalm 17:7, "Wondrously show me Your love for me." Commit to pray your prayer, **DAILY**, for the next thirty days.

CHAPTER 2

"The greatest happiness of life is the conviction that we are loved – loved for ourselves, or rather, loved in spite of ourselves."[8]
—Victor Hugo

"To be fully seen by somebody, then, and be loved anyhow – this is a human offering that can border on the miraculous."[9]
—Elizabeth Gilbert

Jesus was fully human. We easily understand that Jesus was/is fully God because we've seen the miracles, especially His resurrection from the dead. It is much more difficult to wrap our minds around the fact that Jesus was fully human. "For we do not have a high priest [Jesus] who cannot sympathize with us in our weakness, but rather we have [One who has experienced all of life as we have, yet without sin]..." (Hebrews 4:15, changes are my translation). Jesus Himself never sinned, but he did experience the consequences of sin when He bore our sin on the cross. So, Jesus has experienced all of life like we do, as fully human.

That means that He too shared with us the same great desire in life to be fully known and loved (as stated by Victor Hugo above).

When Jesus submitted Himself to John's baptism (at about age thirty, by the way), which many consider the beginning of His public ministry, the Father spoke over Him in an audible voice. The Father did not say something like, "Now, Son, fulfill the mission for which you were born to live." The Father didn't commission His leadership of the people as He did for Moses or Joshua, saying something like, "Be strong and courageous. Do not tremble. Do not be dismayed. For the LORD your God is with you wherever you go" (Joshua 1:9). The Father didn't call Him by a name given for His purpose, something like, "You are The Savior of the World. Now, go and be true to Your calling."

Instead, the Father spoke over Jesus meeting His greatest need and desire, "You are my Son: I love you; and I'm so proud of you" (Matthew 3:17, my paraphrase). The Father established Jesus' identity, from which He would minister for the next 3 years: His Beloved Son. Our identity is who we really are, in our deepest place. From our identity springs every thought, motive, emotion, intention, value, word, and action. Jesus was NOT primarily a miracle worker, nor what people said about Him, nor His titles (The Christ, Messiah, The Son of Man, Savior), nor His power over Satan. He was primarily the Beloved Son of His Father.

Immediately after establishing Jesus' identity, the Spirit led Him into the wilderness where He was "tempted" by the devil (Matthew 4). The temptations were many-faceted but included a direct attack on Jesus' identity as the Beloved Son of His Father. How would He be known? How would He define Himself? Who would He play to in order to be successful?

When the devil said to Jesus, "…command that these stones become bread" (Matthew 4:3), he was in essence saying to Him, "You are (your identity is built around) what you do (it's usually our first question getting to know someone at a party. "Now, what do you do?"). You are what you accomplish. Be known as a miracle worker."

Then the devil took Jesus to Jerusalem and had Him stand on the pinnacle of the temple and challenged Him to "…throw yourself down; for it is written…" (Matthew 4:5-6). The devil was referring to Psalm 91, which says the angels will catch Him. Now that would be spectacular. Everyone will speak well of Jesus. You are (your identity is) what others say about you.

Finally, the devil "took Jesus to a very high mountain, and showed Him all the kingdoms of the world, and their glory; and he said to Him, 'All these I will give to you, if you fall down and worship me'" (Matthew 4:8-9). This attack on Jesus' identity was framed with, you are what you have power over, what you control, what your position is.

Jesus was able to turn away from these powerful lures, which were seeking to define Him by the standards of the world, because He knew He was loved by the Father. That was what defined Him. That formed His identity from which He would minister.

Everything Jesus said or did grew out of His knowing that He was the Father's Beloved Son.

Jesus knows us, through and through, which means He knows our deepest need. No one knows our hearts better than Jesus. Jesus knows we need the exact same foundation for our identity from which we shall live. To that end, Jesus speaks over us in John 15:9, "As the Father loves me, that's how I love you. Now, make your home in my love for you" (my translation).

These 3 phrases in John 15:9 establish the truest thing about us, who we really are, our identity.

"As the Father loves me…" We use words to describe God like omniscient, omnipresent, all the omni[10] words. That makes His love omni-love. We know God as infinite, beyond measure. That makes His love

infinite love. Can we agree that's a good love, the best of loves – The Father's love?

"…that's how I love you." That same love, omni and infinite love, is Jesus' love for us. How do we know this love is for us (since we cannot hear an audible voice)? Jesus explains, "Greater love has no one than this: that one lay down his life for His friends…No longer do I call you servants…but I have called you friends..." (John 15:13, 15). Paul also explains, "But God demonstrates His own love toward us, in that while we were still sinners, Christ died for us" (Romans 5:8).

"Now make your home in my love for you." The Greek word *meino* is most often translated as *abide* or *remain*. But at its heart, it means "to dwell there, permanently." So, to translate the verse, "to make your home" in Jesus' love for you is not a stretch. Your home is where you are accepted for who you are; there is no need to present an image to be liked. Your home is where you share life with your family, not having to measure your words, knowing all are "for you." Your home is your safe place where you go to rest, let your guard down, be encouraged, gain perspective and support, be cried with, laughed with, and celebrated with, and most importantly, be loved just as you are (not as you or others think you should be). Making your home in Jesus' love fills you up before you go out into the cruel and harsh world, that in many ways tries to tear you down.

Jesus establishes your identity in John 15:9: you are primarily the beloved son/daughter of Jesus.

For a woman, the idea of being loved, adored, and cherished makes perfect sense to grow into. Jesus' love meets the deep longing in a woman's heart. But for a man, growing into Jesus' love may seem a bit more foreign.

As a kid, when I dreamed about what I wanted to be when I grew up, it certainly didn't include: I want to be the beloved son of Jesus. No, I wanted to be a fireman, a professional athlete, etc. As John Eldredge says, "…deep in his heart, every man longs for a battle to fight, a beauty to rescue and an adventure to live."[11] How does that line up with being the beloved of Jesus?

Think about Jesus. He absolutely was a warrior who fought many battles against the prevailing culture, even clearing the temple court, overturning money tables, and driving out the livestock with a whip. He fought His greatest battles with the second most powerful person in the universe, Satan himself.

Jesus rescued many a beauty in His day, including adulteresses, traitors to their people called tax collectors, thieves, people possessed by demons, people considered unclean, children of soldiers and rulers, just to mention a few. And He rescued all of us, His image bearers, from the throes of sin.

What an adventure Jesus lived. Walking on water, teaching multitudes, healing every disease, confronting the oppressive religious structure, etc. Then, in the giving of His very life on the cross, His purpose is fulfilled by becoming the Savior of the world.

Jesus' fighting, rescuing, and living an adventure-filled life all sprang from His identity as the Beloved Son of His Father. Jesus was not primarily what he did or what He accomplished, He was not primarily what others said about Him, or primarily His position, even as Savior. He knew, in His deepest place, He was, first and foremost, the Beloved Son of His Father.

The same is true for us who have attached ourselves to Jesus, become His followers, and surrendered our hearts and lives to Him.

Remember the apostle John referring to himself five times in his Gospel (John 13:23, 19:26, 20:2, 21:7, 20) as "the disciple whom Jesus loved." That's just how he knew himself.

We too, can know ourselves in the same way. We no longer have to present to others a self to be accepted or applauded. We can recognize and surrender to Jesus our "false self" that we have created in order to survive or to be successful. We won't strive for, or be enslaved by, a need for wealth or position. We no longer have a need for others to know all we've done or be known by what our job is. We are set free in many ways to be less self-focused and more other-focused.

How can we continue growing into knowing our belovedness in Jesus? Can I really know myself as "the disciple whom Jesus loves"?

First, a reminder of this reality:

It takes time to grow into Jesus' love for you... You don't microwave yourself into an identity of being the beloved of Jesus. Richard Foster calls it the slow work of God in your heart.[12] Again: I am the beloved of Jesus, and I'm still growing into my belovedness. Grant yourself grace.

Exercise 2

I read the other day that we hear, and our brain can process, 60,000 voices a day in our heads, and that 45,000 of them are negative. A counselor friend told me she often finds herself saying to her clients, "You've got to get your self-talk right," meaning you've got to speak the truth to yourself. Let truth (not lies or what is false) be the dominant voice you hear.

As that relates to growing into Jesus' love and our belovedness, create your own Beloved Charter.[13] A Beloved Charter is verses from God's word (no human words) that speak to how The Father, Jesus, and the Holy Spirit see you and think of you. Nothing drops into our hearts like God's very Words.

On the next page is my own Beloved Charter. You may use it, change it, add to it, or delete from it. Or you can start from scratch and write your own Beloved Charter. The important thing is: make it your own personal Beloved Charter.

Then, here's the challenge:

Read it out loud every day, slowly, for the next thirty days.

Pray it as you read it.

Doing this will help you get your self-talk right. You are speaking the truth, reality, to yourself. With the help of Jesus and His Spirit from within our hearts, you will grow more into Jesus' love for you. Of all the exercises, the Beloved Charter has helped me the most grow into Jesus' love.

Beloved Charter

Your Name, the truest, most real thing about you is that you are My Beloved Son/ Daughter (Luke 4:22; John 1:12; 1 John 3:1). **I formed your inward parts and knitted you together in your mother's womb. You are fearfully and wonderfully made** (Psalm 139:13-14) **in My Image** (Genesis 1:27), **made a little lower than the angels, and crowned with glory and honor** (Psalm 8:5). **You're the apple of My eye** (Psalm 17:8) **and I delight in you every day** (Psalm 16:3; 18:19; Proverbs 8:30). **You are My Beloved...My Desire is for you** (Song of Solomon 7:10). **I have called you by name; you are Mine. You are precious in my sight and honored, and I love you** (Isaiah 43:1,4). **My Love for you is the best part of life** (Psalm 63:3). **Just as the Father has loved Me, that's how I love you. Now, make your home in My Love for you** (John 15:9). **Nothing, I promise, will ever be able to separate you from My Love for you in Jesus** (Romans 8:38-39).

You did not choose Me; rather, I chose you (John 15:16; Ephesians 1:4; Psalm 65:4). **Let's live together as friends/companions** (John 15:13-14). **I am with you every moment of every day of your life** (Matthew 28:20). **I gladly give you My Spirit** (John 16:7). **With Him, I lead you, guide you, and am writing a beautiful story of your life as you trust Me** (John 10:3-5; Proverbs 3:5-6; Psalm 16:11; John 10:10). **In Me, live, and move, and have your very being** (Acts 17:28). **I am committed to your happiness and fulfillment, and to your wholeness, nothing less** (John 15:11; Philippians 2:13; Ephesians 1:3, 2:10; Galatians 4: 19, 5:22-23; Matthew 4:19).

Above all, know always, I am for you (Romans 8:31; Psalm 56:4,9)**; and, be assured in your innermost place, of My relentless Love for you** (Ephesians 3:14-19; Psalm 23:6). **I am, and My Love for you is, the Rock on which you can build your life** (Matthew 7:24-27).

CHAPTER 3

"The first objective of discipleship is to bring apprentices to the point where they know in their deepest place Jesus loves them, with no catch."[14]
—Dallas Willard

We know Peter as the brash disciple who often opened his mouth to insert his foot. During the last meal with His disciples, Jesus, trying to share with them again what is about to take place that very evening, says, "You will all fall away because of Me this night, for it is written, 'I will strike the shepherd, and the sheep of the flock shall be scattered.' But after I have been raised, I will go ahead of you to Galilee" (Matthew 26:31-32).

The disciples still weren't getting it.

Peter speaks up, "Even if they all fall away because of You, I will never fall away…Even if I have to die with You, I will not deny You!" (Matthew 26:33, 35).

As we know, just a few hours after his big declaration of loyalty and faithfulness at all costs, Peter fell asleep when Jesus, in great distress, asked him specifically to "…keep watch with Me" (Matthew 26:38); and then, Peter denied he even knew Jesus three times when confronted by two servant girls and a bystander.

According to Luke, after Peter's third denial and a cock crowed, Jesus turned and caught eyes with Peter. Peter immediately remembered how the LORD told him that he would deny him those three times. "And [Peter] went out and wept bitterly" (Luke 22:62).

Peter had not kept his grand promises to Jesus. He had totally let Jesus down at His hour of greatest need. Peter was devastated. Then, Jesus died. Jesus was gone.

Mary Magdalene, Mary (the mother of James), and Salome came to Jesus' tomb after the Sabbath to anoint Jesus' body. They found the stone rolled away and an angel telling them, "…[Jesus] has risen... But go, tell His disciples *and* Peter, 'He is going ahead of you to Galilee; there you will see Him, just as He told you'" (Mark 16:1-7, emphasis mine).

Meanwhile, Peter and a few disciples were in Galilee and went fishing. That night, they caught nothing. An unrecognized man called out to them from the beach to cast their net over the right side of the boat. For some reason, they do it, like ten feet will make a difference. The net filled with more fish than they could haul into their boat. Peter's mind must have raced toward a previous catch of fish (almost three years before in Luke 5:1-7). As Yogi Berra said, "It's Deja-vu all over again."[15] The apostle John identifies the man on the beach, saying to Peter, "It is the Lord!" (John 21:1-11).

Remember, Peter had just resisted Jesus washing his feet, fell asleep while Jesus was in anguish, and denied that he ever knew Him. Wouldn't you think that he might be hesitant to face Jesus again? That he'd lower his head and slink like a dog knowing he'd done wrong? That he would hang back, wondering when Jesus would summon him forward, apprehensive about what Jesus would say to him?

Are you surprised at all that when Peter hears that the man on the shore is the resurrected Jesus, he cannot even wait for the boat to row ashore? He immediately dives into the water and swims to shore. He makes a beeline for Jesus.

How do you explain Peter's dash to be next to Jesus?

The only explanation that makes sense is that during Peter's three years with Jesus, he grew to know that Jesus loved him, no matter what. Peter knew in his deepest place that Jesus loved him "without caution, limit, boundary, or breaking point" (as Brennan Manning said)[16] and Jesus' love satisfied the deepest longing of his soul. The chance to be close to that love again meant more to him than life itself (Psalm 63:3).

What draws you to Jesus? Is it that you believe He's real and promises you heaven? Or is it that you believe there is actually a hell, and it scares you to Jesus? Or is it His unconditional love, which is granted to you, not based on anything you do, nor is it diminished by anything you've done?

According to the apostle Paul God's love (Jesus' love) draws us to Him.

"…The kindness of God leads you to repentance?" (Romans 2:4).

"But when the kindness of God our Savior and His love for mankind appeared, He saved us, not on the basis of deeds which we did in righteousness, but in accordance with His mercy, by the washing of regeneration and renewing by the Holy Spirit" (Titus 3:4-5).

You might sum up Martin Luther's concept of conversion like this, if a man is converted because of fear of any kind (hell, death, punishment, etc.), he will eventually hate his conversion; but if converted because of love, he will grow to love his conversion and want to grow into it.

If you come to Jesus because you know you are loved by Him, you'll want to keep growing into knowing His love and your belovedness as the most true thing about you. All of your life will spring from Jesus' love. You like Peter can learn to live loved.

CHAPTER 4

"What comes into our minds when we think about God is the most important thing about us…the most portentous fact about any man is not what he at a given time may say or do, but what in his deep heart conceives God to be like."[17]
—A.W. Tozer

As St John of the Cross teaches, the soul must consent to divine love – allowing the overwhelming Lover to enter and transform the deepest center of our being.[18]

Paul David Tripp says that he is persuaded that much of our fear, anxiety, discouragement, hopelessness, and difficulty in trusting God is the result of a bad or weak view of who God is.[19]

The Renovare Institute offers courses, retreats, podcasts, a book club, essays, etc., to help people grow spiritually. They teach to always begin with what they believe is the most important question for a follower of Jesus to answer: What is your view of God?

Even a child's first question when they begin learning about God is, "What is God like?"

Every one of us develops a view of God from our life experience, our family, teachers along the way, friends, our culture, our reading, maybe some church-going, etc. A view of God emerges (not necessarily in our consciousness) that truly reverberates throughout our living, our perception of life, and our interpretation of events happening in the world and to us. Our view of God is lodged in our hearts.

God is often seen as passive in our world today, letting things take their course. He can be seen, influenced by the Star Wars movies, as an impersonal force. Our natural bent, left unchecked, tries to define God and tame Him, so as to manage how He works in our lives. It's been said that God made us in His Image and we return the favor, i.e., make God into our image of Him.

Who should we turn to as we discern our view of our God? We turn to God to reveal Himself.

The Bible (God's very word) offers several ways we can view and relate to God. All of them are valid.

- God is the Good Shepherd, and we are His sheep (Psalm 23; John 10:11-18)
- God is "my Lord and my God" as Thomas confessed to Jesus (John 20:28), and we are His faithful servants (Romans 10:9; Philippians 2:11; 1 Peter 3:15)
- God/Jesus is our Creator (Colossians 1:16), and we are His creatures, created beautifully and uniquely in His Image (Genesis 1:27)
- God is a King and a Judge (Matthew 25:34-46), who holds our eternal destiny in His Hands, and we are His subjects living to honor our King
- God is our Father, and we are His children (John 1:12; Matthew 7:9-11)
- Jesus calls us His friends; He invites us to live in a friendship with Him (John 15:13,15)
- Jesus is the Bridegroom, and we are His bride (Luke 5: 34-35)

The view of God that is most often least considered, and seldom gravitated to, is that of God as our Divine Lover, and us as His beloved. However, this view of God might be the one most dominant in the Scripture.

When God chose this tiny group of people known as the Hebrew Nation, through whom He would reveal Himself to the then-known world, He gave them a credo describing how to view Him. It was as if He was saying, "This is how I want to be known. Teach your children this credo and let them teach their children." It appears first in Exodus 34, beginning in verse 5. This happens when Moses went up Mount Sinai for the second time to meet with God and receive the two stone tablets with the Ten Commandments:

> Then the LORD came down in the cloud and stood there with [Moses] and proclaimed His Name, the LORD. And He passed in front of Moses, proclaiming, "The LORD, the LORD, the compassionate and gracious God, slow to anger and abounding in love and faithfulness, maintaining love to thousands, and forgiving wickedness, rebellion, and sin..."
>
> —Exodus 34:5-7 NIV

We could summarize His declaration with this: "I want to be known as your Divine Lover...Live today in My love and live out your day in response to My love."

During the years of the Old Covenant, God sent the Hebrew Nation prophets to be His mouthpiece, to speak for Him. We most often associate prophecy to the prophets, where they foretell future events, but they also anointed and advised kings, spoke warnings and pronounced judgment, and exhorted the people to return to God when they strayed. Above all, in and through their words, whether a major prophet or a minor prophet, was the message from God of His unchanging and everlasting love for His people.

Here are a few excerpts from the Old Testament:

Isaiah's words, though spoken nearly 3,000 years ago, are still valid for us today, as God has not changed.

> *"Do not fear, for I have redeemed you; I have called you by name; you are Mine!...you are precious in My sight...you are honored and I love you..."*
>
> —Isaiah 43:1, 4

The prophet Jeremiah speaks from a place of affliction:

> *"I have loved you with an everlasting love; therefore I have drawn you with lovingkindness"*
>
> —Jeremiah 31:3

> *"Yet this I call to mind and therefore I have hope. Because of the LORD's great love [for us], we are not consumed, for His compassions never fail. They are new every morning; Great is [God's] faithfulness"*
>
> —Lamentations 3:21-23 NIV, my additions

God told the prophet Hosea to go marry Gomer, a known prostitute. She will violate their marriage and continue to prostitute herself, but God asked Hosea to stay faithful to her and love her in her failing. This was to be an example to Israel of God's abiding love for them.

> *"I will betroth you to Me forever; Yes, I will betroth you to Me in righteousness and in justice, in lovingkindness and in compassion, I will betroth you to Me in faithfulness"*
>
> —Hosea 2:19-20

Zephaniah speaks of Israel's restoration like this:

> *"The LORD your God is in your midst…He will exult over you with joy, He will renew you in His love, and quiet you with His Love, He will rejoice over you with shouts of joy"*
>
> —Zephaniah 3:17

The largest book of the Bible is The Psalms, often referred to as Israel's Prayer Book. There are one hundred and fifty Psalms (prayers offered). One hundred and seventy-five-times God's Love for us is mentioned, making it the major theme of the Psalms.

King David wrote as many as one-half of the one hundred and fifty Psalms. Wouldn't we love to have the title that is attributed to him: A man after God's own Heart? The fact that he was a flawed man, far from living a perfect life, should be an encouragement to us, as we pray for a heart that longs for God's heart. David wrote Psalm 63 when he was stranded in the wilderness of Judah, far away from family, in the form of a prayer:

> *"Your unfailing love [for me] is better than life itself…"*
>
> —Psalm 63:3 NLT, my addition

More from David:

> *"Your Love for me will relentlessly chase after me for the length of my days"*
>
> —Psalm 23:6, my translation[20]

> *"If I should say, "My foot has slipped," Your lovingkindness [for us], O LORD, will hold me up"*
>
> —Psalm 94:18, my addition

> *"O Israel, hope in the LORD; For with the LORD there is lovingkindness [for you], and with Him, is abundant redemption"*
>
> —Psalm 130:7, my addition

> *"Your lovingkindness [for me]… will continually preserve me"*
>
> —Psalm 40:11, addition mine

> *"I will rejoice and be glad in Your lovingkindness [toward me], because You have seen my affliction; You have known the troubles of my soul"*
>
> —Psalm 31:7, my addition

We could look at many more from the Psalms.

Psalm 90 was written by Moses; it's the first Psalm ever written:

> *"Satisfy us in the morning with Your lovingkindness [for us], that we may sing for joy and be glad all our days"*
>
> —Psalm 90:14, my addition

Solomon wrote several Psalms and The Song of Solomon, which is the story of a Lover seeking after his beloved. It's an allegory picturing God as the Lover and we as His beloved.

> *"He has brought me to His banquet hall, and His banner over me is love"*
>
> —Song of Solomon 2:4

> *"I am my beloved's, and his desire is for me"*
>
> —Song of Solomon 7:10

God, throughout the history (which is His-Story) of the Hebrew nation, continued to identify Himself and remind His people, "I am the One who loves you. Please receive My love and live into it, and out of it."

Of Jesus, it is recorded in John 1:18 that "no one's ever seen God at any time, but the only begotten Son [Jesus], who is in the bosom of the Father, He has explained Him [has made him known, has revealed Him]" (additions mine). And Jesus loved people like no one had ever seen before or since. He embodied love, living out the Exodus 34:5 revelation of who God is.

This is very important.

Because if we have never considered our view of God as our Divine Lover, as the God who loves us, then we are in danger. This is also the case if we once believed Jesus loves us, but that view has faded in the mundane routines of life, or if we have doubted that view of God in the hard things (suffering) that life throws at us. The danger is that we could slowly gravitate to what I call a Santa Claus view of God: "he sees you when you're sleeping; he knows when you're awake; he knows if you've been bad or good, so be good for goodness sake."

If this view (or variations of it) lodges in our hearts, we will have little hope to live loved.

Exercise 3

Let's say after a hard day of physical labor in your yard: planting, gardening, putting out mulch, edging, trimming, mowing, etc., instead of the normal shower, you choose a hot bath. You ease yourself into the tub, letting the water cover you. As you are soaking, you totally release your muscles to relax. Reflect on what your view of God is. Perhaps, you could even imagine God's love for you as the bath and let yourself rest, soak, and bask in it, for today! Psalm 46:10 says, "Be still, and know that I am God!" I would add to that, "Be still and know that I am the God Who loves you… for real."

CHAPTER 5

"The greatest honor we can give Almighty God is to live gladly because of the knowledge of His love [for us]."[21]
—Julian of Norwich (my addition)

"Have you been seized by the power of God's great affection?"[22]
—The slave community around in New Orleans, circa 1800-1850.

What is the mark of one who is a disciple of Jesus? Is it their commitment, above all else, to Jesus, willing to give their very life, like a kamikaze pilot was to their country and cause in WWII? Is it one who is becoming more like Jesus (Romans 8:29; 2 Corinthians 3:18)? Is it their increasing knowledge of the Scriptures and of theology, and their engagement in ministry for Jesus? All these are valid.

But the people I know who exude the aroma of the joy and peace that comes from knowing Jesus (2 Corinthians 2:15-17), who live with ease a life full of love, and who seem to be free from the things that hold others captive, are all people who know they are loved by Jesus.

They are people like the person most often referred to in the Bible as "the anointing woman."

Of Jesus' encounter with this woman, He says, "'… wherever this gospel is preached in the whole world, that also which this woman has done shall be spoken of in memory of her'" (Mark 14:9). Full stop…mic drop. What a momentous declaration! What is the message for us?

The "anointing woman" with Jesus is included in all four Gospels: Matthew 26: 6-13; Mark 14: 3-9; Luke 7: 36-39; John 12: 1-8.

Who was this "anointing woman"? Matthew, Mark, and Luke don't give her a name, but Luke does identify her as an immoral woman, a sinner. This designation was given to a prostitute, an adulteress. John says the "anointing woman" is Mary, the sister of Lazarus. This makes sense, as the Synoptic Gospels have placed this encounter in Bethany, which is where Lazarus' family lived.

Could it be that the woman who anoints Jesus is the same woman who was caught in adultery, in the very act, who the Pharisees threw at Jesus' feet in the temple demanding she be stoned to death for her adultery (John 8:1-11), as the Jewish Law commands (Deuteronomy 22:22)?

The Synoptic Gospels record the event taking place at the home of Simon the Leper, a Pharisee himself. For sure, Simon was no longer a leper, or he wouldn't be at his home hosting a dinner. It would make sense that Simon had been healed by Jesus, and he was hosting a "thank you" celebration. Perhaps, he was the leper healed in Mark 1:40-42 and Luke 5:12-14.

Simon's meal was interrupted by this immoral woman. Was she invited? Doubtful. Did she sneak in? Probably. Imagine the intrusion, the total disruption of a dinner party.

The perfume which she used to anoint Jesus was pure nard. Spikenard is an extract from a flower that only grows in the Himalayas. During the encounter, the perfume is said to be worth three hundred denarii. A denarius was a day's wage; three hundred denarii was considered one year's wage. The median income in the United States in 2020 was $41,535. That's expensive perfume worth a year's earnings…a $41,000 jar of perfume? Who would have a jar of that expensive a perfume? A high-class prostitute could have had it.

The aroma of the perfume would have filled the house, overwhelming the smell of the meat being cooked or the bread being baked. All conversation stopped; the room fell silent. Everyone turned to watch this woman and Jesus. How long before someone spoke? Ten minutes…fifteen minutes…?

Matthew and Mark record her anointing beginning with Jesus' head, as the coronation of a king would be. Luke and John record her anointing beginning with Jesus' feet, as a servant would perform. She was weeping. Her tears fell on Jesus' feet, and she wiped them off with her hair.

Either way, the prostitute's "touching" Jesus made Him unclean by the Jewish code of law. Add to that, a woman only let her hair down for her husband. It was considered immoral to have such a public display of affection as she anointed Jesus. Scandalous, to say the least.

For the people at the dinner, the whole scene must have been difficult to process. Then Jesus makes His profound declaration: "Wherever you share My Gospel, you tell this woman's story," adding even more to their confusion.

What is Jesus asking His disciples (and us) to take notice of? Is it her humility? "Humble yourselves before the Lord, and He will lift you up" (James 4:10 NIV). Is it her act of worship and adoration? Jesus said, "…if they [the people] keep quiet, the stones will cry out" (Luke 19:40 NIV, addition mine). Is it her abandonment unto Jesus, her complete denial of herself, and total surrender to Jesus? "If anyone wishes to come after Me, he must deny himself and take up his cross daily and follow Me" (Luke 9:23). Is she preparing Him for His upcoming burial, which she couldn't have known at this moment in time (Mark 14:8)? All these beautiful possibilities are true enough to make Jesus excited.

Here's what I think.

For Jesus, she represented a snapshot of the Gospel He had been communicating for His three years of ministry. Jesus was essentially saying, "My Gospel is that I love you, regardless of who you are, where you've been, or what you've done. Will you let me love you? If you receive/accept My love into your innermost being, I will heal you of any brokenness and free you of anything that holds you prisoner, and forgive your sin. This woman *'gets'* Me. She's received My love, and she's simply loving back. You tell her story."

A prostitute would have a lot of experience with distorted love, counterfeit love, and manipulative love. She had heard spoken words of love too many times to count. Words with no heart and no authentic meaning behind them. She would be able to discern genuine love. Of all people, she would know when she'd been loved for real. When she came in touch with Jesus loving her, the inventor of love loving her, she was overcome. She was "seized by the power of God's great affection."[23] She embraced, received, and was filled with His Love. The anointing was her responding with her best love. The apostle John, in his first letter, in essence says that we love God because He first loved us (see 1 John 4:10, 16, and 18). Jesus: "Tell her story."

For Jesus, the "anointing woman" is a picture of what the Gospel can be for us. She knows her belovedness in Jesus: she's let it seep over time into her innermost being. She's just responding with her life. She's not grinding out obedience to live the "the Christian life," rather, she's simply loving back.

If we don't know ourselves to be deeply loved by Jesus, our living "Christianly" or "for Him" is just duty or compliance or our effort with good works to win His Favor. Jesus doesn't want our compliance. He wants us to know ourselves as His Beloved and to live our lives in response to His Love. Like this woman: Tell her story.

Paul says in 2 Corinthians 5:14, "For it is Christ's love that compels us" (my translation). The Greek word we translate "compelled" is *sunecho,* and it means to be "pressed in upon," or "so compressed that there's only one way you can move." The Passion translation of this verse uses the phrase: *"fuels our passion."* What Paul is saying is that knowing Jesus' love is the greatest influence on his thoughts, words, motives, and actions.

All of us are compelled by something; it's what motivates us or moves us to action. For example, for some it's the desire for success or the pursuit of some achievement or the need to be liked, etc. For the anointing woman, it's experiencing Jesus' love for her that presses in on her heart and moves her. Simply put, she (or the person) who is loved much, loves much. Jesus: "Tell her story."

The anointing woman knows she is loved with no catch. She is loved beyond her mistakes, her bad choices, and her hurt. As Jesus' love for us seeps from our minds into our hearts, we know we're still His beloved even when we fail. Deeper than our woundedness and frailty is our identity as Jesus' beloved. "This woman knows that. Please tell her story when you speak My Gospel," Jesus says.

She's not deciding, "Do I give 10% of gross or net income?" She's been loved extravagantly, so she's loving extravagantly. Brennan Manning once said that maybe when we meet Jesus face to face after this earthly life, He might ask us just one question. "Did you believe I loved you? That I desired you? That I longed to be with you?"[24] I want to answer, "Yes Lord, and I lived my life, though imperfectly for sure, absolutely motivated in response to Your love for me." Maybe this is another aspect of Jesus saying for us to tell this woman's story wherever we share His Gospel of Love.

Doesn't she put on display the true freedom that seems so elusive for us? She doesn't care what others think about her as the disciples scold her. She's not performing for Jesus, trying to get Him to respond in a certain way. When you grow into Jesus' love for you, the things that we long for to be true of our lives that we see in her can actually be true for us too. Jesus: "Tell her story."

The first rule of discipleship is: Let yourself be loved by Jesus. Then, once you receive Jesus' love, you enter the lifelong journey of happily growing into Jesus' love and your identity as His beloved son/daughter. Your life becomes simply loving Him back, responding as one who is living loved.

It's as if Jesus was saying: "Whenever you speak of My love for you and share of my death which reconciles you to God, and joyfully speak of My Resurrection and of being alive and "with you always", include My encounter with the anointing woman. She totally *'gets'* Me."

CHAPTER 6

"The love of Jesus for you and me is not a mild benevolence or a sentimental kindness, but a consuming fire."[25]
—Blaise Pascal

"I can better contain the Gulf of Mexico in a shot glass than comprehend the wild, uncontainable love of God for me."[26]
—Brennan Manning

If someone said that you could be filled with "all the fullness of God," how would you respond? Is that even possible? Would you wonder what the catch is? Or would you respond with some intrigue, "Tell me more." The apostle Paul, who wrote most of the New Testament, makes that very claim and shares how it can be a reality for us. The reality of being "filled with all the fullness of God" is directly related to our growing into Jesus's love.

The pinnacle of Paul's letters has to be Ephesians 3:14-19.

It begins, "…I bend my knees before the Father, from whom every family in heaven and on earth derives its name..."

In Paul's day, prayer was done standing. Even Orthodox Jews today stand and rock as they pray. When people came to Jesus, they bowed before Him, whether lepers (Mark 1:40), Jairus the synagogue ruler (in Mark 5:22), even Satan, who called himself Legion (Luke 8:28). Remember, Paul had written earlier the great hymn recounted in his letter to the church at Philippi that one day every knee will bow at the name of Jesus (Philippians 2:10). So, Paul is bowing for this prayer. It reminds us to also come before God in humility.

Paul is coming before God as his Father. Jesus invited us to pray that way, even addressing the Father as "Abba," the intimate term "daddy." And he's beseeching the One from which all of us originate. "Name" in the Bible doesn't mean our given name, but it denotes our whole person, our character, our essence. All of us were first a thought in the mind of God, way before our conception. "…He chose us in Him before the foundation of the world" (Ephesians 1:4). That's the Father to whom Paul is praying.

Then Paul prays for us, "…that He would grant you, according to the riches of His glory, to be strengthened with power through His Spirit in [your innermost place]…" (Ephesians 3:16, my translation).

All of life, all we are, all we experience, is a gift from God. It's like James, the brother of Jesus, said, "Every good thing bestowed and every perfect gift is from above, coming down from the Father of lights…" (James 1:17). It's like the Father says to the older son in Jesus' The Extravagant Father parable, "All that is mine is yours" (Luke 15:31).

Yes, that "The Father would grant us…" a gift to us from His Glory? His Glory – His Magnificence, Beauty, Dignity, Weightiness. In Exodus 33:18-23, we read how Moses got very comfortable with God, talking with Him as with a friend. But then Moses overstepped in his comfortability. He asks God to show him His Glory. God responds that, of course, no one can see His Glory and live. Paul is asking for a gift from God's Glory.

Here comes the beginning of the heart of Paul's prayer: That in our innermost place, in the depth of our being, our soul, where we are most "us," in our very heart, we'd be strengthened with power by His Holy Spirit at work in us (Ephesians 3:16, my translation).

When we trusted Jesus with our lives and became a follower of Jesus, by virtue of Jesus' death on the cross, our sin was removed, forgiven, washed clean (Titus 3:4-5), and we were/are reconciled with God. Wow, so good, deep breath. But that's just the beginning. We are now on the journey of transformation, and we cannot transform ourselves on our own. We need to be empowered by the Holy Spirit to grow and change. Jesus never expected us to live a Christian life, or to be transformed on our own strength. He knows "the spirit is willing, but the flesh is weak" (Matthew 26:41). So He gave us His Spirit. And the Spirit can accomplish the deeper realities of our faith, which includes a heart set free as we grow into Jesus' love.

We don't usually associate "power" (the Greek word is *dynamos*) with being a believer. Isn't it more about being meek and mild, turning the other cheek, and washing each other's feet? Paul's talking here about the power of the Resurrection, the power of the Holy Spirit at work in us. Wow, Glory.

Paul continues, "so that Christ may dwell in your hearts as you trust Him…" (Ephesians 3:17, my translation). The phrases "Christ in you," or we are people "in Christ," are used over 100 times in the Bible. But this is the only place that speaks of Jesus dwelling in our hearts. The Greek word we translate "dwell" is *katoikeo*. It means to settle down permanently, not like the Bedouin roaming, setting up their tents in each new place when they decide to stop for a while. Jesus' indwelling our hearts is not a temporary assignment. It's permanent…forever…no matter what.

In the Bible, "heart" means the center of our being. The heart is not just the seat of our emotions, but rather it is the command center. In Romans 10:9, Paul says we must "believe in our hearts that God raised Jesus from the dead."

So, the prayer continues with, "with Jesus settling down permanently in the center of our being as we trust our lives to Him, we could be rooted and grounded in His love for us…" (Ephesians 3:17, my translation).

Rooted in Jesus' Love. At my Chapel Hill, North Carolina home, we had Bermuda grass, which is a runner-type grass. A section of my lawn was burning out, drying up, while the rest was flourishing. Upon investigation, I found that the grass roots over time had grown around and over the sprinkler head in that section of the yard, and the sprinkler head couldn't pop up and water the grass. That's our being rooted in Jesus' love, like the sprinkler head is being rooted, totally surrounded, circled around, overgrown by Jesus' love.

Grounded in Jesus' love. I had a friend living in San Francisco whose home's foundation cracked during an earthquake. Insurance would not cover the damage because his home was not bolted to the foundation.

So, he had to pay to have his home literally bolted to his foundation going forward. That's being grounded upon Jesus' love, just like my friend's home being bolted to the foundation; our hearts are bolted to Jesus' love.

Paul's praying we'd be overcome, rooted in, and bolted upon, Jesus' love for us. So that, "…we may comprehend with all the saints what is the breadth and length and height and depth, and to know the love of Jesus which surpasses all human knowledge…" (Ephesians 3:18-19).

Comprehend. That we'd be able to understand and believe without any doubt that Jesus loves us, to grasp it for ourselves, to make it our own.

It is a love that cannot be measured. *Breadth* – for every person. *Length* – went to such lengths as to die on a cross to make the way for His love to be poured out into our hearts. And the length includes that it lasts forever, for all eternity; it never fades nor fails. *Height* -- Jesus loves us from heaven and higher still. It's infinite love. *Depth* – Jesus loves even the most degradable sinner. We never deserve Jesus' love, nor can we earn Jesus' love.

To know the love of Jesus (and to grow into the love of Jesus). What does it mean "to know" Jesus' love?

The Greek word *ginosko,* which we most often translate as "know" in English, means so much more than know *about*, or give intellectual assent to, or have knowledge of. It even means more than to believe or accept to be true. *Ginosko* means "to have union with" – "to become one with."

John chapter 17 is Jesus' prayer with His disciples the evening before He gave His life for them (for us). He prays: "And this is deep, rich, lasting life, that you would *ginosko* the one true God and Jesus Christ whom He has sent" (verse 3, my translation). The life we so desire is not found in knowing about God, or even in believing and aligning our lives with Jesus' teaching. The life we desire is found in becoming one with Jesus and His love.

Jesus' love surpasses any human knowledge. Think of the best love you've ever seen, heard about, read about, or seen in a movie, or experienced yourself. Jesus' love doesn't compare to anything we know as humans; it by far surpasses it.

So, when you grow into Jesus' love, "you will be filled with the fullness of God" (Ephesians 3:19, my paraphrase).[27]

Wow. Growing into Jesus' love for us can yield for us, being "filled with all the fullness of God." I'm trying to think of something better than that, and I'm at a loss. I just can't think of anything better.

Exercise #4

Let us join with Paul and pray this prayer, **daily**, during the month of your birthday. Maybe memorize it so as Psalm 119:11 (KJV) says, "Thy Word have I have hidden in mine heart."

Ephesians 3:14-19

"…I bend my knees before the Father, from whom every family in heaven and on earth derives its name, that He would grant you, according to the riches of His glory, to be strengthened with power through His Spirit in [your innermost place], so that Christ may dwell in your hearts through faith [as you trust Him]; and that you, being rooted and grounded in [His] love [for you], may be able to comprehend with all the saints what is the width [breadth] and length and height and depth, and to know the love of Christ which surpasses [all human] knowledge, that you may be filled to all the fullness of God." (additions mine)

CHAPTER 7

Drawing on decades of ministry and personal suffering, Tim and Kathy Keller argue that suffering lies at the heart of why people disbelieve and believe in God, of why people decline to grow in character, of why God becomes less real and more real.[28]

"In The Song of Solomon, God is depicted as pursuing the soul as His beloved. The fathers of the Church have a fondness for this particular verse: 'O that his left hand were under my head and that his right hand embraced me' (Song of Solomon 2:6). According to their interpretation, God embraces us with both arms. With the left He humbles and corrects us; with the right, He lifts us up and consoles us with the assurance of being loved by Him. If you want to be fully embraced by The Lord, you have to accept both arms: the one

that allows suffering for the sake of purification
and the one that brings the joy of union
[with Jesus' love]."
—Thomas Keating, (addition mine)[29]

"In the world you have tribulation, but take courage;
I have overcome the world."
—Jesus (John 16:33)

The Bible contains 32,000 promises (yes, someone counted them). When God promises us something in His Word, we can take it to the bank of our heart, deposit it there; it is ours. Of the 32,000 promises, not one of them is that life will go the way we want it to go and that we will never encounter any form of suffering. None of us escapes pain in this earthly life. Bad and hard and even unjust things will happen to us. Jesus says so in John 16:33 (above). By the way, the Greek word translated *tribulation* is *lipsis.* It means "be crushed like a grape."

Our personal suffering can be from life just wearing us out. We're not sure we can keep going. We're frayed, fighting off anxiety, with despair creeping in, and negativity gaining ground, all causing us to question things we were certain of before, like: does Jesus really love me? Or, our suffering can be quite severe, even rivaling the *lipsis* of Job (the Bible's Job), whose wealth is gone, ten children killed, his body covered with boils that are infected with worms, and his wife urging him toward denouncing God and committing suicide, all of which have him totally doubting God's love for him.

This chapter does not offer a theology of suffering, nor attempt to answer the inevitable question accompanying suffering, "Why God?" (which every one of us has asked). This chapter attempts to relate suffering to our growing into Jesus' love, rather than our distancing ourselves from Jesus' love. Because knowing our belovedness in Jesus *does offer us* the way through our suffering, to persevere and even "live well" in our suffering.

In Chapter 12, we'll speak of how Jesus, in His love for us, not only enters into our suffering, but actually bears it with us. He doesn't love from a distance; rather, He takes it on Himself (see Isaiah 53:4).

The Apostle Paul writes in Romans 5:1-5:

> Therefore, having been justified by faith, we have peace with God through our Lord Jesus Christ, through whom also we have obtained our introduction by faith into this Grace in which we stand; and we exult in the hope of the glory of God. And not only this, but we also exalt in our tribulations [*lipsis*] knowing

> that tribulation brings about perseverance; and perseverance, proven character; and proven character, hope; and hope does not disappoint, because the love of God [Jesus' love] has been poured out within our hearts through the Holy Spirit who was given to us. (Additions mine)

First, Paul reminds us of the reality of our relationship with God, whether or not we feel that relationship while we are in the throes of our suffering. The reality is: no one is able to snatch us out of the Father's Hand (John 10:28-29). With Jesus, we can have peace, knowing we stand in His grace. We may be clinging to Jesus with white knuckles from within our dark place, but we are connected to Him. Paul continues on to say that our *lipsis* (tribulation) is developing our character. Then, Paul shares the solid foundation under us, in us, and through us; that is, God's love/Jesus' love, which is being poured out into our hearts by the Holy Spirit. In our knowing we are Jesus' beloved, we never lose hope. It is hope and our being loved that carry us in the midst of our suffering.

Viktor Frankel, who survived three years in the Nazi concentration camps, wrote in his book *Man's Search for Meaning*, that the moment a fellow prisoner lost hope, it was a short time until they died.[30] Hope for us is fueled by our knowing Jesus' love.

For me, when I went through the biggest heartbreak in my life (which is too long a story to write about at this point), it wasn't Ann's (my wife's) words attempting to bring reasoning into the story that helped me through it, or even her words of comfort. It was her love and her hugs. I needed to know I was still loved and believed in.

Paul further speaks of Jesus' love and our belovedness in Jesus as he concludes what many consider Paul's Gospel: Romans chapters 1-8.

If you were commissioned to write your version of The Gospel of Jesus, what would be your last sentence capturing the essence of the Gospel? Here's Paul's summary sentence: "For I am convinced that neither death, nor life, nor angels, nor principalities, nor things present, nor things to come, nor powers, nor height, nor depth, nor any other created thing will be able to separate us from the love of God that is [ours] in Christ Jesus our Lord" (Romans 8:38-39, addition mine).

Wrap your heart around that reality: we can never be separated from Jesus' love.

Our pain is very real; it can be consuming and defining. By suffering's nature, it takes center stage in our lives. I am not putting a smiley face on our being squashed like a grape by offering a glib platitude about Jesus' love, nor am I exhorting anyone to be some victorious Christian claiming their belovedness overcomes their tribulations. I am saying our pain and suffering do not disqualify or negate Jesus' love. I am saying being "the disciple whom Jesus loves" is a greater reality in the midst of our suffering. Though knowing our belovedness in Jesus doesn't guarantee we won't suffer in our fallen world, what it does guarantee is that Jesus will give us Himself; we will always stay connected to him; and we will experience His love being poured out into our hearts. Yes, suffering actually grows us more into Jesus' love.It has me. I would never know the extent of my belovedness in Jesus unless I had gone through *lipsis.*

CHAPTER 8

"For of His fullness we have all received,
and grace upon grace."
—The Apostle John (John 1:16)

A teacher at a Christian college asked her class of thirty students: "I don't want to know what your particular sin is; what I want to know is how you think Jesus views you in the midst of your sin."

She received the following responses:

- He's really disappointed in me.
- He expects better of me.
- He's angry because He hates sin.
- I know I'm not what God wants me to be.
- God speaking: "Don't you see how this is hurting you and grieving Me?"

Not one student said, "He loves me."

An aside: Even right away in the Garden of Eden after Adam and Eve's "sinning", God shows His continued love for them in giving them skin for clothing (covering) and in still pursuing them, "Where are you?"

I don't know of any encounter Jesus had with a person that reveals the very heart of God, like the following one. And this encounter speaks to what might be the greatest hindrance to our growing into Jesus' love:

> *And early in the morning He [Jesus] came again into the temple, and all the people were coming to him; and He sat down [a rabbi's position] and began to teach them. And the scribes and the Pharisees brought a woman caught in [the act of] adultery, and having set her in the midst [center of the courtyard], they said to Him, "Teacher, this woman has been caught in the very act of committing adultery. Now in the Law, Moses commanded us to stone such women; what then do You say?" And they were saying this to test Him, in order that they might have grounds for accusing Him. But Jesus stooped down, and with His finger wrote on the ground. But when they persisted in asking Him, He straightened up,*

> *and said to them, "He who is without sin among you, let him be the first to throw a stone at her." And again, He stooped down and wrote on the ground. And when they heard it, they began to go out one by one, beginning with the older ones, and He was left alone, and the woman, where she was, in the center of the courtyard. And straightening up, Jesus said to her, "Woman, where are they [your accusers]? Did no one condemn you?" And she said, "No one, Lord." And Jesus said, "Neither do I condemn you; Go your way. [And leave this way of life that is so harmful to you]."*
>
> —John 8:2-11, my additions

It doesn't take a deep-feeler with a great imagination to enter into the overwhelming humiliation and embarrassment that was heaped upon this woman. She was thrown in front of Jesus and the crowd to be stoned for adultery. To say she was afraid doesn't come close; she was experiencing sheer terror. The Scripture tells us that she was caught in the very act. Do you think the ones setting the trap for Jesus allowed her to get dressed or even grab a sheet to cover herself? I doubt it. She must be cowering in a fetal position with her head buried in her arms, awaiting what appears to be her final moments before her death.

The most educated religious minds, the lawyers, Pharisees, and the high priest all came together to create their best trap yet to discredit Jesus. Jesus was heralded as a better teacher than they were, and Jesus, being a Jew, said that He did not come to abolish the law but to fulfill it (Matthew 5:17). The law to the Jewish nation was like our Constitution is to the United States; it was their nation's identity. But Jesus was known for His compassion for known sinners; He was called the Friend of Sinners.

So, you see, they had Him cornered. If He lets the crowd stone her, He upholds the law but shows no compassion and forgiveness of sin that He is known for. If He forgives her and stops the stoning, He disrespects the law, which clearly states in Deuteronomy and Leviticus to stone those who commit adultery.[31] What would Jesus do? How will He get out of this one? His mind must be racing to find a way.

So, Jesus stoops down and begins writing in the dirt. Why? Some say He's buying time to think. I say He's taking the attention off this woman who's horrified. Everyone is looking to see what He's writing, thus not looking at the woman. The "trap setters" care nothing for this woman; she's just a pawn in their scheme. On the other hand, Jesus sees a beautiful image bearer scorned, mistreated and abused, and His heart goes out to her.

The teachers press in for a response from Jesus. Jesus brilliantly dismisses the crowd. He begins to speak with the woman. What do you think He would say to her after just saving her life?

He doesn't lecture her on how adultery offends God and is a sin that hurts her life, too. He doesn't ask her if she's sorry for her adultery or if she regrets the lifestyle she's chosen. He doesn't demand a firm commitment to change going forward.

Here's what He says to her: "'Where are your accusers? Does no one condemn you?' And she said, 'No one, Lord.' Then Jesus said, 'Neither do I condemn you; go your way and leave this way of life that is so harmful to you'" (John 8:11, my translation).

Jesus just freely gives her His grace!

If she was afraid, she is afraid no longer. 1 John 4:18 states her reality clearly, "…perfect love [that's Jesus' love] casts out [all] fear" (ESV, my additions). That reality is the same for us.

An aside…

This encounter was not included in the Bible for several centuries. There was never a question of its authenticity or that it actually happened. It wasn't included because it was considered scandalous. The prevailing thought was: you can't tell people there is no condemnation for sinful deeds; if they believe that, they'll go do whatever they want to do. There is no incentive to live well. Over time, Jesus and His grace were more understood (if it ever can be understood). Folks grew to believe that if you really heard Jesus say to you, "I do not condemn you", and you truly received His grace and love, then you'd go do whatever He wants you to do.

Before I accepted Jesus, I did, I thought, and I said some awful, embarrassing things. After I accepted Jesus, I did, I thought, and I said some awful, embarrassing things. You know the Bible says there is nothing hidden that will not be revealed, and nothing spoken in secret that will not be made known (Luke 12:2-3). In fact, if you watched a video of my thoughts, motives, feelings, and actions of just the last two weeks, you would agree with me that I'm totally justified in condemning myself. Self-condemnation, being repulsed by ourselves, and even self-hatred are things that plague all of us to some degree.

The Bible has a word for our self-condemnation: *SHAME.*

Imagine Adam and Eve in the Garden of Eden before the apple incident. They have a grand purpose. They see beauty. They know love for each other. They have a deep connection with God, who meets with them every day in the "cool of the afternoon." How would you describe them and their emotional state in one phrase? How about: they were filled with joy? Or they had a song in their heart? They lived lightly and freely? They had no cares, burdens, or anxiety? No, the phrase God chose to describe them is: "They felt no shame" (Genesis 2:25).

Here's what shame does to us. It goes beyond recognition of bad behavior to say, "What kind of person does that?" or "What kind of person thinks that?" Then shame builds to say, "If you really knew what kind of person I am, you wouldn't want to hang out with me." Shame fans the flame of thinking: "God's got to be disappointed with me, or at least he's frustrated with me."

Shame brings with it feelings of inadequacy, of not being enough, of inferiority, of unworthiness, certainly not worthy of Jesus' love. Shame whispers to our hearts that we are unlovable. Shame and its companions, by their nature, cannot receive Jesus' love. Shame rejects grace, or at least stiff arms it. Shame is a huge hindrance to our growing into Jesus' love.

Often, we are not aware of shaming ourselves. Shame is like an undercurrent running through us, subtly speaking in our hearts and even taking up residence there. For instance, here are some ways I shame myself:

- "I've walked with Jesus over fifty years. I should have made more progress." *Shame.*

- I knew Jesus in college, but I didn't live so well for Him. I have some regrets, and regrets morph into shame pretty quickly.
- "Some of my prayers aren't answered; I must not have enough faith." *Shame.*
- "I've gotten pudgy; folks must think I have no self-discipline." *Shame.*

There are many more. These are just a few I can share publicly.

How do we handle our shame?

Left on our own, we hide or repress within ourselves our shame, so no one can see it. Often, this bubbles up and leads to self-hatred. What might be redeemable, we try to fix.

But if we can learn to recognize what brings shame upon us, and then name it, shame is brought into the light. Then, consciously in prayer, we can bring our shame before Jesus. As Romans 8:1-2 says, "There is therefore now no condemnation for those who are in Christ Jesus. For the law of the Spirit of life in Christ Jesus has set you free from the law of sin and death."

You know, it's one thing to know and believe the great theological truth stated above by the Apostle Paul; it's quite another thing to have Jesus look you in the eyes and hear Him say to you, "I do not condemn you.," like He spoke to the adulterous woman.

Here's the reality. Of course, Jesus knows what kind of person I am; yet, in total knowledge of all I've done or thought, He sees beyond my flaws to the very best of me and says, "I do not condemn you; now, let's go do life together."

Here's Jesus' plan for our shame; it's clearly stated in Hebrews 12:2: "…for the joy set before Him [Jesus] endured the cross, [bearing our shame]…" (additions mine). Our shame is removed from us and placed on Jesus on the cross.

In the South, we have an expression. When someone does or says something stupid or just plain wrong, it is said, "I can't believe you did that (or said that) …shame on you." Instead, the grand reality is that Jesus, in His grand love for us, says, "I can believe everything you've said and done, now, shame *off* you. On the cross, it was joy for Me to absorb all your shame; so now, in Me, you have no condemnation…Shame off you. Receive My love."

Jesus knows all about our fears, our failures, our brokenness, and wounds that we hide from others and have a hard time facing ourselves. He doesn't expect us to be perfect. He knows we'll mess up. But, we must know this, it is joy for Him to live in our hearts. We have His love. We always will. So, we stop accusing ourselves. Shame off us. We receive Jesus' grace and love into our innermost being and continue to grow in our belovedness.

Exercise #5

In Jesus' love and with the Holy Spirit's help, begin to recognize shame in yourself. How do you shame yourself? What causes you to subtly move toward shaming yourself? Write them down. It helps clarify those things and bring them into the light. Then read Hebrews 12:2 and give your shame to Jesus. It's His joy to take shame off you and onto Himself.

CHAPTER 9

"Your beauty and love relentlessly chase after me every day of my life."
—King David (Psalm 23:6, my translation)

"Jesus loves you, Leif. He's on your side. He's coming after you. He is relentless."[32]
—Leif Peterson (from his dad's eulogy)

Many people say, "If only I could hear Jesus say to me in an audible voice, 'I love you' (like Jesus heard Himself at His baptism), then I could truly believe it."

Where do we turn to know Jesus loves us for real? Where can we hear Jesus say, "I love you"?

All of us at different times are overwhelmed at the beauty we see in Jesus' creation…in what we call nature. "Everything was created through him; nothing – not one thing – came into being without

Him" (John 1:3-4 MSG). A sunset, a seahorse, a daisy, watching the Discovery Channel or National Geographic capturing a beautiful animal or landscape, seeing something big and fantastic like the Grand Canyon, or something smaller like each uniquely made snowflake--all (and so much more) remind us that Jesus made all this from love.

As Psalm 33:5 says rightly, "The earth is full of God's unfailing love for us" (my translation). Or as Eugene Peterson's *The Message* says, "Earth is drenched in God's affectionate satisfaction." All of earth's beauty is filled with God's/Jesus' love; it all has His imprint. Then comes the most beautiful of Jesus' creation…His masterpiece…not just with His imprint, but with His very image. You and me.

You and I were born out of Jesus' love. It's our original love. We were loved before any person loved us on earth. We were made for Jesus and His love to fill us. We are accepted by Him, no matter what family, culture, other people, environment, or life experience might communicate otherwise.

When you take a walk by yourself (of course, you are not alone, but accompanied by the risen, alive Jesus), you begin to notice the warmth of the sun, maybe a gentle breeze, all the different shades of green,[33] and birds being playful as they chase each other. If you look closely in one square yard of the ground, you can see it teeming with life: ants, small bugs you can't name, etc. All made with such design and love.

While walking in God's creation, you may sense that you are in God's presence. At times, you may hear, like Elijah did (1 Kings 19:12), Jesus' gentle whisper, what many call today: a still, small voice. You may not make out exact words, but you can tell that it's a voice of love. And you sense you are a part of that love.

C.S. Lewis' *Screwtape Letters* is about Wormwood, Satan's assistant on earth, who is assigned a backslidden Christian. Wormwood is to keep the backslidden Christian backslidden. But he fails. The backslidden Christian comes back into his faith. Satan scolds Wormwood, pointing out his mistake: allowing the patient to take solitary walks, because those walks unexpectedly brought the man into contact with reality, nature, and God.[34] With all the distractions held at bay when we take a walk with Jesus, we become attuned to our being held in His great love story. We are the ones loved.

In addition to Jesus' original love for us and His still, small voice, we look at Jesus on the cross. Jesus is screaming from the cross: "Please know I love you!"

Isaiah 53:5 (NIV) says:

> But he [Jesus] was pierced for our transgressions, he was crushed for our iniquities; the punishment that brought us peace was on him, and by his wounds we are healed.

Why is Jesus on the cross? "…for the joy set before Him, He endured the cross…" (Hebrews 12:2). What is the joy for Jesus? His joy is a deep, love relationship with you and me. He's on the cross to remove the only barrier between His love and us. We must see Jesus on the cross as more than His great rescue and the fixing of our sin problem.

We can also see and receive Jesus' love at the cross: "I am the good shepherd; the good shepherd lays down His life for the sheep. No one has taken it [My life] from Me, but I lay it down on My own initiative… Greater love has no one than this, that one lay down his life for his friends…You are my friends…" (John 10:11,18; 15:13-14).

Jesus' rescue to love us takes place on the cross when Jesus said just before he died, "Father, i*nto Your Hands I commit My Spirit*" (Luke 23:45), and then, "*It is finished*" (John 19:30). At that moment, something cosmic, huge, even mysterious happened, but very real. Jesus bore our sin and all its consequences (the shame, self-condemnation, alienation from God, etc.)

on Himself. He actually became sin. He cried out, "My God, My God, Why have you forsaken me?" (Matthew 27:46) as He experienced the alienation from God that we do because of our sin. At that same moment, Jesus transferred to us His righteousness. 2 Corinthians 5:21 says it well, "He [God] made Him [Jesus] who knew no sin, to actually become sin, that we might become the righteousness of God in Him." We are presented before God "holy and blameless, as you stand before him without a single fault" (Colossians 1:22 NLT).

I call it *The Great Exchange.* God did for us what we could not do for ourselves. The barrier or blockage between us and God's Love for us (our sin) has been destroyed. It had to be Jesus, the Perfect One, to bear our sin, or there is no rescue. No other person could declare that they are going to die for us and their death make any difference for our sin.

Under the inspiration of the Holy Spirit, in God's Word, all the verses that describe our condition of sin and its effect on our lives, also describe Jesus' rescue… in the very same verse. It's incredible. It's like God couldn't wait to tell us of His provision after He described our mess. It shows His heart's desire for us not to be estranged but to be united with Him in a love relationship. Each reality – the reality of sin, the reality of our rescue, and the reality of Jesus' love being ours--are only separated by a comma. I call it The Glorious Comma:

> *"For all have sinned and fall short of the glory of God [comma], being justified as a gift by His grace through the redemption which is in Christ Jesus"*
>
> —Romans 3:23-24

> *"For the wages of sin is death [comma], but the gift of God is eternal life in Christ Jesus our Lord"*
>
> —Romans 6:23 NIV

> *"We all, like sheep, have gone astray, each of us has turned to our own way [comma], and the LORD has laid on him [Jesus] the iniquity of us all"*
>
> —Isaiah 53:6 NIV

> *"And although you were formerly alienated and hostile in mind, engaged in evil deeds [comma], but He has reconciled you in His fleshly body through death, in order to present you before God holy, blameless, and beyond reproach"*
>
> —Colossians 1:21-22

The cross is the signature of Jesus. This expression "the signature of Jesus" comes again from Brennan Manning in Abba's Child…where the context is him sharing the crucified Christ is the definitive revelation of God's love. It's the ultimate expression of His love for us. When someone dies for you, you no longer question if they have good intentions towards you, or if they love you.

The cross tells me three things:

1. Something is more wrong with me than I thought…meaning my sin and its effect in my life and in my heart is huge and cannot be overcome on my own strength.
2. I am of more value than I ever thought… meaning that God would give His own Son to die on my account, for my good.
3. I don't have to wonder if God wants me or loves me. He would do anything for me to be with Him.

In what might be the most recognized Bible verse, John 3:16, don't get lost in "the world" in that verse. Rather, you must put your name in its place:

> *"For God so loved* **[your name]** *that He gave His only begotten son, that whosoever puts their trust in Him can have [deep, rich, lasting life]"* (my translation).

Don't ever think that Jesus' love for you stops at the cross. It is a present-day reality, with you, pursuing you, every moment of every day.

In Jesus, we can see God's heart; He puts it on display. "No one's ever seen God at any time, but Jesus…Who's in the very bosom of the Father, has made Him known (or has explained Him)" (John 1:18, my paraphrase).

The Hebrew word for the verb used in Psalm 23:6, (quoted at the beginning of this chapter), is *radaph*, which means "to relentlessly pursue." God and His Son took the initiative with us, based on grace and grace alone. Jesus pursues us even into His suffering and death. That is the greatest love. Even though Jesus relentlessly pursues us with His love, it's not a straight trajectory upward of our knowing it for ourselves. Often it feels like two steps forward and three steps back, or like a roller coaster with its ups and downs.

Even in the Song of Solomon, where the bridegroom (God) is pursuing his beloved (us), it is a journey of ups and downs. Sometimes the bride is left desolate. Sometimes she seeks him but can't find him. She calls, and he doesn't answer. We see her wandering in the street, in the wilderness, searching in the garden, then in Lebanon, then in the fields, then in the house. At times, she is deeply aware of her unworthiness. But always, she believes in her heart that she will hear the voice of her lover, of her beloved, and she's assured again of his faithfulness to her. She knows she is chosen, and is beautiful in his sight. She knows she is his beloved. This, too, is our journey into Jesus' love.

Jesus is the great respecter of us image bearers; He never takes away our choice. So, the human condition requires this of us: if we deeply desire to know ourselves as "the disciple whom Jesus loves", we must choose every day to follow that desire and ask for the Spirit to help us grow into Jesus' love and to grow Jesus' belovedness in us. It's a choice we must make every day.

CHAPTER 10

My Story

"Let your religion be less of a theory and more of a love affair."[35]
—G.K. Chesterton

"Of all the Christians I know, most readily assent to Jesus loves them, but only a handful really quite believe it."[36]
—A.W. Tozer

I was a self-absorbed, pretty normal teenage boy when I went on a week of Young Life summer camp and asked Jesus to come into my heart. Growing up in a Christian home, I could have recounted many Bible stories and knew about Jesus' crucifixion and resurrection, but I never heard that Jesus wanted a friendship with me, where He lives in my heart, or that we can do life together. It was an easy decision to accept Jesus, but it did not come easy to live true to my new commitment.

Through my senior year of high school and my four years of college, I lived with one foot in the Kingdom and one foot in the world. It wasn't pretty. I could see the Father, Son, and Holy Spirit having a conversation about me. It went something like this: One said, "Wow, Ty again? I think it's time we let him go. Let him experience the full extent of His choices." Another saying, "I know we hate to give up on anyone, but he's crossed the line too many times." And the Other saying, "We love him so, and there's still a part of him that knows that…he'll come around; can you see the plans we have for him?"

God did hold on to me and I am forever grateful.

In my twenties, after college, I saw that the way I was living was not life-to-the-full at all. So, I threw myself headlong into life with Jesus with all my being, and I loved it. I got involved with Young Life as a volunteer, fell in love with kids, and had a whole new group of friends. The sport of handball brought joy to me as well. Life was good.

At age twenty-eight, still single, I made the decision to go to seminary for one year. Taking a year-long leave of absence from my job, I headed off to Gordon-Conwell Theological Seminary. It wasn't a degree I sought, but adding some "meat to my faith" was my desire. It was a glorious year that changed the trajectory of my life. I met my wife and discerned a call to bring Jesus to kids, not just as an avocation like I was doing, but as a vocation. I joined the Young Life staff.

Truly taking it one year at a time, I continued on the Young Life staff for thirty-four years. There were numerous roles and four moves. Long story shortened, we have three beautiful sons (gifts from God), now all married to wonderful daughters-in-law (answered prayers, each one), and five grandchildren and counting.

From as early as I can remember, I have been controlled by an addiction. I deeply needed to be admired, respected, honored, and applauded. Everything I did and said played to that goal. For many years, that wasn't in my consciousness; it's just how I lived. I was not aware that my desperate need was compelling me.

I built my identity, and presented the image to others, of a person who was funny – so fun to be around, of a spiritual man seeking Jesus passionately, of an up-and-coming leader who ran a successful ministry, and of a handball champion (and much more). Living with my addiction, I compared myself to others who were more gifted than I was. I desperately wanted to be a speaker like ______ (the name is irrelevant); be a leader like_______; play handball or golf like ______; pray like George Mueller (who had 46,000 answered prayers recorded in his journals found after he died); and be deeply spiritual like Henri Nouwen, or the desert fathers. The list goes on. The burden of carrying all these and building them into my presented image was growing heavier and heavier.

By my mid-to-late thirties, I became more aware of my addiction. I'd catch myself saying something, then thinking, "That's not what I believe. Why would I say that?" Or sometimes I'd realize I just told a lie to present myself in a positive light; so you'd think I'm ____ (spiritual, funny, other-centered, or whatever). In so many ways, I was performing, keeping up the image, which was so tiring.

By God's grace, two things happened that changed my life and enabled me to begin breaking free of the control of my addiction. We had a son, our firstborn, and I met Brennan Manning.

There was a daily occurrence in my home that became the new paradigm in my friendship with Jesus.

When Jac (our oldest son) was maybe four to six months old, Ann would put him in his walker – a seat with wheels. Adjusting his seat height so that his feet touched the floor, he could motor around the house (hardwood floors with the rugs pulled up). The scene: Ann's preparing dinner, Jac's in his walker, and my car pulls into the driveway. Hearing my car, Jac would position himself in sight of the front door. I opened the door and as we caught eyes I said, "I'm gonna get you."

Jac's whole face turned into a smile of utter delight; he squealed and turned to run. After a little running, he'd stop and look back to see if I was coming. Of course, I was coming. "I'm gonna get you!" He'd run again but not as much. Finally, he'd stop, because he wanted to get got. I'd hug him, "zerbert" his neck, telling him again and again, "I love you, Jac," and kiss him all over. While I was loving on my son, something deeper was penetrating my own heart. I'm convinced that's how Jesus wants to relate to me (to us).

During that same time, I heard Brennan Manning speak, read his books, and participated in four (four-day) solitude retreats that he led. I'd never heard someone, before or since, speak about Jesus' love for me/us like God through Brennan did. My thirst for Jesus' love, and my being captured by His love, became my reality. I, over time, released and scraped any other identity or image that I had created and even enjoyed. I traded them in to be "the disciple whom Jesus loves."

You've heard of Charles Wesley. He and his brother John attended Oxford University and while there, they formed the "Holy Club." They were committed to studying the Bible and living a holy life. Their leadership led to what became known as the Methodist movement, the beginnings of the Methodist denomination.

In 1735, the brothers left England for the thirteen colonies, to engage the colonists in Georgia for the purpose of evangelizing them. They failed miserably. They were mocked, shot at, and eventually run out of Georgia by Governor Oglethorpe himself. Completely defeated, Charles came back to England deathly sick and emotionally unhinged. He was depressed and even his faith was lost. During his nearly two years in the hospital, a Moravian by the name of Peter Boehler visited him regularly, almost daily. Through his care, his words, and prayers, Charles came to know Jesus.

Charles Wesley called his coming to Jesus at that time, his conversion. He would say that previously he knew the Bible, could articulate the Gospel, was involved in ministry, but that he never had a personal love encounter with Jesus. He said, "I had preached faith and Christ to others, but had not yet myself experienced the assurance of God's love."[37]

Though my story is certainly not nearly as dramatic, I could have written those last two sentences about myself and my experience of Jesus' love.

I've reflected on why it wasn't until my late thirties that I became aware of my addiction and wanted to address it. Maybe I was like those in Jesus' encounter with the Pharisees and the adulteress woman where those that were the older ones dropped their stones first. Do we have to have some road go under our wheels (i.e. mature) before being able to see within ourselves? Maybe it was because I had some success with my presented image; God blessed my ministry, folks thought well of me, I won some handball championships, etc. Maybe it was all in God's perfect timing? Maybe Jesus' love had to travel that long journey of one foot between the head and the heart, and it's the heart that dictates much of our lives lived. "The good person out of the good treasure of his heart brings forth what is good…for his mouth speaks [and his body acts] from that which fills his heart" (Luke 6:45, addition mine). "Watch over your heart with all diligence, for from it flows the springs of life" (Proverbs 4:23). It probably was a combination of all of the above.

Then came the latest gift from God: being asked to leave Young Life staff, and in a very hurtful way. It further thrust me into Jesus' love and my belovedness in Him. Any remaining tentacles of my identity being in ministry with Young Life were severed. My belovedness in Jesus was all I had, happily so. Who was it who said, "You never know Jesus is all you need until Jesus is all you have"? I'd add to that to personalize it to me: "You never know Jesus' *love* is all you need for your identity until Jesus' *love* is all you have." I wish I had the right words to express my gratitude in being set free from the control of desperately needing you to think I'm so neat…the right words to capture the joy of being full of Jesus' love and living out of that love. Set free by God's Grace and His Spirit in me to Live Loved.

CHAPTER 11

As I continue growing into Jesus' love, here are a few things I am experiencing as I live loved:

- Psalm 46 begins, "God is our refuge and strength. A very present help in any trouble. Therefore we will not fear, though the earth should change, and though the mountains slip into the heart of the sea" (verses 1-2).

  Then it builds, "The Lord of hosts is with us; The God of Jacob is our stronghold." (verse 7).

  It finally reaches its pinnacle with verse 10 of the Psalm, "Cease striving [Relax…Let go] and know that I am God" (addition mine).

  I would add and amend that last line with the reality of, "and know that I am Jesus who loves you."

When you get up in the morning and know that Jesus loves you…that you are fully known and still loved…that no one cares more deeply for you today than Jesus, the One who "upholds all things by the word of His power" (Hebrews 1:3)…that Jesus' love has "got" you today--you can live loved! Then you relax and let go. There's nothing to be anxious about. Jesus, in His love, will continue writing a beautiful story of your life today. "My boundary lines have fallen in pleasant places" (adapted from Psalm 16:6 NIV).

I heard a golfer interviewed after he just missed an eight-foot putt on the final hole to finish in second place in a tournament he had led the whole final round. He blew the lead. When asked how he was feeling, he responded (not exact words), "I get to go home to my wife who loves me, and my three-year-old son whose face will light up when he sees me. He'll jump into my arms and kiss me. He doesn't care if I finished in first or in fifty-sixth place."

Living loved by Jesus is like that for me. He loves me if I've had a good day or a messed-up-by-my-fault day. So, I can live lightly and freely. I can take risks. I'm not protecting myself. I'm not uptight. Living life with Jesus, I find myself relaxed in His presence. I'm fully known and accepted in Jesus' love.

- This is the big one for me. My addiction to needing to be liked, applauded, heralded, and lifted up…always doing my best to present the created image toward that end…*is gone.* I've exchanged that old image for my real identity as the disciple whom Jesus loves. All my striving to uphold that old image no longer controls me. Oh, it rears its head every now and then. But I recognize it more readily, put my arm around it as an old friend, and tell it, "Sorry. You have no place here anymore. I am the Beloved of Jesus."

Accompanying being freed of my addiction, I've noticed that:

1. I don't feel the need to share all my accomplishments (so-called). God's already delighted in me (Psalm 18:19; Proverbs 8:30). That's enough.
2. I'm not burdened with meeting other people's expectations of me.
3. I no longer grasp for others' affection, and strangely, I grasp less for things of this world that previously I thought I needed for more life.
4. I experience less envy or jealousy. And the hell of comparing myself to others is gone. Jesus loves me, just as I am.

5. There's no fear creeping in of rejection or of not being a part (1 John 4:18). In fact, fear has little say over my actions. Jesus' love for me impels and empowers my actions.

- When you live loved (by Jesus), you're no longer gritting your teeth and grinding out obedience to Jesus's teaching and commands with sheer determination, trying so hard to show your good works to others that they might praise their Father in heaven (Matthew 5:16). Now, I'm living by responding to Jesus' love for me. I'm loving back. His commands seem easier, like gracious invitations to more life.[38]
- Knowing I am loved by Jesus, no matter what, I have more courage to face and confess my sins, my falling short. Being loved by Jesus, I accept myself more readily. I'm human and in the process of transformation (Psalm 103:14; Matthew 26:4; Philippians 2:13). I have no need to shame myself or hide part of myself from Jesus. I am fully known and fully loved. The flip side of that same record is that I have more desire to dig deeper into my shadow side, the parts of me that hinder wholeness, and the places that need healing. I pray Psalm 139:23-24 with more boldness: "Search me, Oh God, and know my

heart; Try me and know my anxious thoughts [my mind]; And see if there be any hurtful way in me, And lead me in the everlasting way [Your way]" (additions mine).

- In general, living loved, I'm aware that I love others differently, namely, more or better. The best I can explain is that the self-life (that is, where it's all me and not God) takes a back seat. I am more interested in the other person. The person who is loved much, loves much.
- As David says in his Psalms:

"For You are my rock and my fortress; For Your name's sake You will lead me and guide me… I trust in You, O LORD… My times are in Your Hand" (Psalm 31:3, 14-15a).

"I trust in Your love for me; My heart rejoices in Your salvation (which You have bestowed upon me). I sing to The LORD because He has dealt bountifully with me" (adapted from Psalm 13:5-6).

"How precious is Your love for me, O God. Your children take refuge in the shadow of Your wings. They drink their fill from the abundance of Your house. You give them to drink from the river of Your delights. For with

You is the fountain of life" (adapted from Psalm 36:7-9a).

"I trust in the LORD's love for me, forever and forever" (adapted from Psalm 52:8).

"Let me hear Your love in the morning, for I trust in You" (adapted from Psalm 143:8a).

In short, we trust a person to the extent we know we are loved. I find myself trusting Jesus more as I grow into His love. I'm trying to control my circumstances less and less. I am confident in Jesus' love and goodness that He's writing a better story of my life than I could ever dream up for myself. I am not passive by any means; I'm more attuned to the Spirit in my activity. Overall, I am more content with my life.

- I'm not as anxious or stressed. In Jesus' love, I know deeply that He's "got" me.
- I've learned that Jesus' love for me is not because I've presented my best traits before Him, proving myself worthy of His love. Jesus isn't attracted to me because of my "loveliness" (He's actually attracted to me because of my neediness). In short, Jesus' love for me is not because I have value; rather, Jesus' love for me creates my value.

I ran my first race in Charlotte, North Carolina. It was called "JK Polk's Fun Run." It was an eight-mile run from Southpark Mall to JK Polk's birthplace. I'd lived in Charlotte for fifteen plus years and had never visited JK Polk's birthplace. When I got to the finish of the race, JK Polk's birthplace was about an acre of land on which stood a one-room dilapidated log cabin. I realized it was basically "nothing." What gave it its value was a president of the United States lived there. Same with me/us. What gives me/us value is that the Creator and Sustainer of the universe loves me and lives in my heart.

- Again, I wish I could explain this one: I am just more grateful. Thanksgiving comes more frequently and easily as I am being loved by Jesus and living loved with Him.

Who wouldn't want any of those things to be more real in their lives? You know the saying: that if something seems too good to be true, then it's probably not true. Well, Jesus' love for us is true, and His desire for us to know ourselves as His beloved son/daughter is true, and His Spirit's growing in us a deeper knowing of our belovedness in Jesus is true, even though it all seems too good to be true!

CHAPTER 12

There's a beautiful word in the Greek that our English translations of the Bible have difficulty capturing its full meaning. It is a verb used to describe how Jesus loves us. It appears twelve times in the Synoptic Gospels (Matthew, Mark, and Luke).[39]

Let's consider the event recorded in Luke 7:11-17. As Jesus is approaching a city called Nain, He encounters a funeral procession leaving the city. The Scripture tells us the dead person was a boy, the only son of a woman who was already a widow. Can you imagine the pain and loss this woman must be carrying? Jesus was being accompanied by "a large multitude," and the funeral procession was a "sizeable crowd." The scene is full of lots of people.

Verse 13 says, "When the Lord saw her, He [*splochnitzomai*] her…" The Greek word is "Splochnitzomai" (Phonetically pronounced: splok-neat-zo-my). What does it mean?

The Greek is a much fuller language than English. The Greek language has many words for "love" depending on the context and the intended meaning. You've heard of *agape,* meaning unconditional love, *eros,* meaning romantic or sexual love, *phileo,* meaning brotherly love, and *storge,* meaning affection. In English, I must use the same word "love" for all kinds of different meanings. I can say, "I love to play golf," or "I love that movie." I look my wife Ann in her eyes, who I've been married to for forty-four years, and say, "I love you, Ann." It's crazy that the same word "love" is used to mean totally different things.

Splochna (the verb) is yet another Greek word for love, a deep, deep love.

When we sympathize with someone, we're saying that we can imagine what they're going through. When we empathize with someone, we're saying that I've experienced something really similar or exactly what they are going through. *Splochna* is deeper than both sympathizing and empathizing.

The root of *splochna* is "*sploch,*" which means the bowels of a person, the deepest place in a person. And from that place, you enter into what the other person is going through and take it on yourself. We love the person so much that we actually bear their pain with them.

The closest example I know of this kind of love was when a friend of mine lost both her mother and father in the same year. Her father had a long battle with Alzheimer's, and during its later stages, her mother was diagnosed with lung cancer. Once, I called my friend after her father had passed, and her mother was declining quickly. I asked her how it was going and how she was doing.

She was explaining the situation, then she said, "Strange thing though. I woke up several nights in a row, unable to catch a breath. I literally felt that I was not going to be able to breathe in another breath. I went to my doctor, who was concerned. He ran several tests but didn't find anything that was able to explain my symptoms. As the doctor and I talked, however, we mutually discerned that in my deep love for my mother, I was taking on her suffering. As she experienced trying to take another breath, so was I struggling to breathe." She so loved her mother from her "bowels" that she was bearing her burden on herself.

Jesus loves us with *splochna* love. Seven hundred years before He was born, the prophet Isaiah spoke of Jesus' love in that way: "Surely He has borne our griefs and carried our sorrows" (Isaiah 53:4 ESV).

Jesus looks at the widow from Nain at her son's funeral and *splochnas* her. Our English cannot translate *splochna* as it should. If we said, "Jesus so loved this widow that as He understood her pain, He entered in and took it upon Himself," of course, that would be too wordy. So, it is generally translated "Jesus had compassion on her," or "His heart went out to her," or, He took pity on her," or simply, "Jesus loved her."

As Jesus *splochna*-ed her, He stopped the funeral procession and raised the young man back to life. The miracle was born from Jesus' *splochna* love for her.

I had an experience with Jesus' *splochna* love that I'll never forget.

I met the father of a teenage girl who was involved in Young Life at the school at which I was leading. He asked to meet me for lunch, over which, he briefly told me his life story. Because he was a workaholic and an alcoholic, he lost his family through divorce and alienation. Through it all, he began a relationship with Jesus and turned his life around. Alcoholics Anonymous also played a big part. He was excited that his daughter had allowed them to reconnect and build a relationship.

He and I became dear friends. I was just becoming aware of my addiction to presenting an image in order to be admired and applauded. I was in the process of becoming freer of its hold on me. I accompanied my friend to his AA meetings several times. I was so attracted to what I saw in the men there. Why? Because they were authentic and genuine. They had any semblance of an image come crashing down as a consequence of their addiction, and they were now their real selves. I wanted that so much.

My friend met a woman, fell in love, and made plans to be married. They asked me to be the officiant, the minister. At the rehearsal dinner, the toasts were all his AA buddies sharing who my friend was to them and how much they admired his journey. It was beautiful.

But I'm sitting there frantically crafting my toast in my head. I was the minister, so I needed to be spiritual. But I needed a little humor because that plays well with a crowd. It's good to be funny. It's important for people to think a minister is fun. I need to share a great story that captures the essence of my friend. Folks like a good story. But I can't go too long because folks will think I'm really into myself. What I was doing was desperately trying to present my constructed image.

While all this is going on in my head, the brother of the bride stands up to give his toast. Robert is his name, and through a small world story, it turns out I know Robert. Robert is mentally challenged; he's much younger maturity wise than his physical age. Robert is the bag boy at the checkout of the grocery store nearest to my house. Often, I'm making a grocery run later at night after our kids are in bed.

As Robert bags the groceries, he comments on many of the items as he puts them in the bag, addressing the buyer. For instance: "Oh, dog food. This is a good one. Your dog will like this. You know, I have a dog." Then he tells the buyer about his dog and asks about their dog. Most shoppers are annoyed and ignore him, but I find myself always going to his line and engaging with him, enjoying the conversation, and trying to affirm him. I didn't know he was related to the bride until that night, at the rehearsal dinner.

Before his toast, Robert stands up, walks over, and directly faces the head table where the bride and groom are sitting (in other words, he's not facing, nor talking to the crowd). Robert says (my best from memory), "Carol (his sister's name changed for this writing), you are a beautiful person. You are the most important person in my life. I would not be where I am today without you in my life. I love you." Then he turns to Tom (name changed for this writing), "Tom, you're getting the gem of the earth." Then he sits down.

As you might imagine, there are tears welling up in every eye in the room. Except for me, I am crying so hard that I'm heaving. My wife tries to put her hand on my shoulder, but I'm bouncing up and down, and it won't stay there. As I'm crying, my mind is racing, trying to figure out why I am crying. I'm totally surprised, maybe even in shock at myself.

Then, it comes upon me. In my growing to recognize my addiction and journeying into being freed from it by knowing my truest self as "the disciple whom Jesus loves," I realized I wanted so much to be like Robert. He wasn't trying to live up to an image that everyone would like; he was just being himself. I was weeping because deep down I knew I had so far to go.

And then, I heard in faith, in my crying, Jesus speaking to me. That still small voice inside, but very clear. He said, "It's okay Ty. I've got you. I *splochna* you. I've got you. It's going to be okay. I understand. I *sphlochna* you." As I came to a calm, there was a peace inside me. I made a huge step into Jesus' love that night and into living loved. I did end up giving a toast; but I can't remember what I said. I do remember speaking from my heart, from my true self, loved by Jesus, and it felt so good.

The love of Jesus, that we are growing into, knows all we are experiencing and enters into our "stuff" and bears it with us. Wonder of wonders, yet true. Invite Jesus right there, into your deepest place. As He comes (doesn't need to be asked twice), He brings freedom from what holds us captive, release from what oppresses us, and healing to our broken hearts (Luke 4:18 and Isaiah 61:1).

CHAPTER 13

"Let this Lover, this tremendous Lover, into your being."[40]
—St. John of the Cross

"The Christian ideal has not been tried and found wanting. It has been found difficult; and left untried."[41]
—G.K. Chesterton

If growing into Jesus' love is so desired (by Jesus and by us) and wonderful, with so many benefits to us, then why is it so difficult?

In my life, and in the lives of others I've been privileged to share life with, there arise many things hindering our growing more into Jesus' love and our "living loved." Things that need to be healed, obstacles that need to be brought into the light and overcome, changes in our awareness and in our coming to Jesus that need to happen, etc. The following highlights some of those things:

- For many, seeing themselves as "the disciple whom Jesus loves" either feels a bit arrogant or out of reach. That designation is for a select few who really give all of themselves to Jesus and His Kingdom. They are other-worldly, holy, having a different make-up or personality, and walking a different path than them.

  However, Jesus' love is given to every image-bearer; being His beloved is for everyone, without distinction. Grace wouldn't be grace if it had criteria for distribution. Truly, we can grow to see ourselves as God sees us, that being "a disciple whom Jesus loves."
- In writing about the adulterous woman thrown in front of Jesus (Chapter 8), we spoke about shame. The feeling that is attached to shame is our unworthiness. And unworthiness by its nature stiff-arms Jesus' love or outright rejects Jesus' love.

  Hebrews 12:2 clearly states how Jesus removes our shame by bearing it on the cross. As we name it, He bears it; it is removed from us. In our world, we put the burden on ourselves to prove we are worthy to be loved by Jesus. But that's not the way it works with Jesus; it's hard to grasp that Jesus bestows His love on us regardless of our worthiness or unworthiness.

- We were taught as kids, "It's better to give than to receive." It has stayed with us. We like "doing love" for others, especially for God. It's easier and provides a bigger return for my goodness than just receiving love. "Doing love" supports how I think I'm doing, that I am a good person. I came across the following anonymous journal entry where a woman wrote what she heard God whisper to her. It hits close to home.

  Nothing brings Me more delight than to love you. But sometimes, child, you seem to have a hard time letting Me love you. It seems easier for you to scurry around doing love than to open yourself to letting Me love you. Do you want to know why? It's because doing love is good for your ego; sitting quietly and receiving love is humbling. Doing love puts you in charge; receiving love means I am the Giver and you are the taker. You find it safer to be the giver than the taker. Doing love is high profile; receiving love is what happens between Me and you in private. Doing love produces tangible results; receiving love has nothing to stack in the warehouse at the end of the day.

Jesus' love cannot be earned; we will never deserve Jesus' love. We must learn to receive Jesus' love that He gives by grace.

- The place where we first experienced love was in our families, and for many of us that love was a distorted love, leaving us with a wounded heart, cautious toward letting ourselves be hurt again by love. If we didn't "attach" safely to love while we were vulnerable as kids, it is difficult to receive and be captured by Jesus' love as adults. In addition, when we are older, very few of us live through love relationships without experiencing some sort of love not returned, or worse, a betrayal. This leaves us treading with extreme caution toward entering in and trusting in love.

  It is Jesus' love (empowered by His Spirit) that brings healing to our broken hearts. Growing into that beautiful balm, Jesus' love, is exactly what we need for our wounded hearts.
- The last line of the great hymn entitled "When I Survey the Wondrous Cross" is: "Love so Amazing, so Divine, demands my soul, my life, my all." Growing into Jesus' love requires surrender. This isn't natural for any of us. We can't give up control easily. We prefer to do life on our own, have what we might call our own freedom. And

we have sworn to protect our hearts at all costs, which makes surrendering them extremely difficult. Can't we just warm ourselves by the fire of Jesus' Love, rather than jumping in, being burnt and scarred forever? Does Jesus' love for us have to be the treasure in the field that we discover and for joy go and sell *everything* we have to possess the field (Matthew 13:44) and the treasure of Jesus' Love?

Surrender isn't optional. It isn't extra credit. It is absolutely necessary to receive Jesus' love and becoming His beloved disciple. As Jesus says, "...unless a grain of wheat falls into the earth and dies, it remains alone; but if it dies, it bears much fruit. The one who loves their life loses it, and the one who hates his life in this world shall keep it to [deep, rich, lasting life]" (John 12:24-25, additions mine). Our difficulty actually surrendering to Jesus' love might be the biggest contributor to G.K. Chesterton's quote at the beginning of this chapter. Jesus' words haunt me sometimes, "Because narrow is the gate and difficult is the way that leads to life, and there are few who find it" (my condensed adaptation of Matthew 7:13-14). Maybe it's our need to surrender that brings that sentence to life.

Francis Fenelon describes surrender not as striving but as resting—like a baby at peace in its mother's arms—held entirely by love.[42]

To help us with surrender, I often pray the following excerpt from Thomas Keating's prayer:

The Welcoming Prayer
(By Father Thomas Keating)

I let go of my desire for power and control.
I let go of my desire for affection, esteem,
approval, and pleasure.
I let go of my desire for survival and security.
I let go of my desire to change any situation,
condition, person or myself.
I open to the love and presence of God and God's
action within. Amen.[43]

After praying The Welcoming Prayer, then you rest in Jesus' love. Like the Psalmist encourages: "Be still [relax, let go, cease striving] and know that I am God" (Psalm 46:10, addition mine).

The real issue, more than believing Jesus loves us without any conditions, is allowing ourselves to be loved. Receiving Jesus' love moves us out of our own control and places us in Jesus' loving control, which is joyous. It is "Living Loved."

God, in His great respect for us, never takes away our choice. We can basically choose from two options: 1. We can choose to live less-loved (by Jesus), not surrender to His great, never-ending love for us, pursuing our own agenda with our own resources. 2. We can choose to open ourselves up to Jesus' love, let Him love us, receive His love into our innermost self, surrender to His love, and live loved (Chapter 10).

- As life happens and our story unfolds, hard things, bad things, and unjust things befall us. When the unfavorable happens, whatever scaffolding our life was built upon collapses. Everything is called into question, including Jesus' love for us. We think things like:

"I'm in a dark place. Once I knew Jesus loves me, but now, that knowing, that feeling, and that peace is gone."

"Life has beaten me up. My heart is broken. There are too many unanswered prayers."

"Jesus has abandoned me. At the time I need Him most, I don't sense His presence."

"To say I doubt Jesus' love for me would be an understatement."

"I've dug myself into too deep a pit. Despair and hopelessness have somehow been glued to my soul/my spirit."

"Jesus loves me is a forgotten memory. I can't forgive myself."

I've tried to speak about our suffering in chapter 7, and how Jesus' love meets us in our suffering.

- Put bluntly, when we sin, AND don't confess it to Jesus, His forgiveness won at the cross is held at bay. Sin can constrict the flow of our sense of Jesus' love, just like standing on the garden hose can constrict the flow of water.

  Knowing we are loved by Jesus, no matter what, gives us the courage to face our failures and bad choices with brutal honesty and bring them to God in confession. His forgiveness, won by Jesus at the cross, freely given, removes that constriction of the flow of Jesus' love into our hearts (1 John 2:1-2a).
- Satan is constantly trying to dismantle our Faith. His mission is to steal, kill, and destroy any sense of Jesus loving us with an unconditional love. There's never a time when our belovedness in Jesus isn't under assault. In what we refer to as The

LORD's Prayer, Jesus urged us to pray"...deliver us from the evil one" (Matthew 6:13). And in His prayer with His disciples on His last night with them before He would be crucified, "...keep them from the evil one" (John 17:15).

Satan's voice bombards us, putting us down and leading us to believe that God is disappointed in us. It's a voice of despair. It will sound like: "your life is a sham...you're not improving; you're getting worse...you just keep on sinning... it's your fault you're in this mess...you know better...good luck working your way out of this one. Your heart is deceitful above all things. You know you need to make yourself lovable, by how you look or by what you accomplish...and you're failing...God is giving up on you."

Satan and his continuous assault is very real...but remember, the most powerful person in the universe, Jesus and His love, lives in your heart.

Listen to Jesus:

"...no one will snatch them out of my hand"

—John 10:28

"Come to Me all who are weary and heavy-laden, and I will give you rest..."

—Matthew 11:28

I will never give up on you, or stop loving you…
"…a bruised reed he will not break, and a smoldering wick he will not quench…"

—Matthew 12:20 ESV

Listen to the Psalmist:

How precious is Your Love for me, O God!
Your children take refuge in the shadow of Your Wings.
They drink their fill from the Abundance of Your House;
You give them to drink from the river of Your Delights.
For with you is the Fountain of Life.

—adapted from Psalm 36:7-9

For as high as the heavens are above the earth,
So great is [His Love toward us] who revere Him.
As far as the east is from the west,
So far has He removed our transgressions from us.
The love of the LORD for us is from everlasting to everlasting…"

—Psalm 103:11-12, 17, additions mine

Letting Jesus' love overwhelm us is difficult. Receiving grace day after day is humbling. It is only by God's grace that we can begin, and continue to, let Jesus love us. Though it cuts against our natural selves, we must accept God's grace and love for our wounded, frightened, broken, sorry selves. "For of His

[Jesus'] fullness we have all received, … grace upon grace" (John 1:16).

When I visit the beach, we leave our windows open to hear the waves crashing on the shore. They never stop; it's continuous…wave after wave, like Jesus' grace upon grace. That's God's grace and Jesus' love for you. You are loved, and loved, and loved. "The steadfast Love of the LORD never ceases; His mercies they never come to an end…" (Lamentations 3:22-23 ESV).

CHAPTER 14

"There is only one sentence people crave in novels: The Maker of all things loves me and wants me."[44]
—Novelist Reynolds Price

Turn around and believe that the good news that we are loved is gooder than we ever dared hope, and that to believe in that good news, to live out of it and toward it, to be in love with that good news, is of all things in this world the gladdest thing of all.[45]
—Frederick Buechner

When we read a novel (or even just a story), or watch a movie, where someone totally undeserving experiences someone loving them with true love, and when that love bestowed upon them is received into their innermost being, and then that love literally changes them right before our eyes, we are deeply moved. Tears or at least moist eyes come easily. Our own hope for love comes forth.

As we learn more about Jesus' love for us, a true love, it arouses or awakens a deep longing that's been written within us; that is, we long to be loved.

* * * * *

Have you watched the movie or seen the stage play, called *Man of La Mancha*? The main character is Don Quixote. He declares to Alphonsa that she is his lady in whose name he will go into battle. But she is the town whore. The wounds of her life experience have her hold at arm's length Quixote's devotion and love declared. Knowing herself (unworthy, unlovable, filled with shame), she spurns his declaration of her as his beloved. In fact, she yells at him, begging him to stop pursuing her. Instead of retreating, he gives her a new name, Dulcinea (meaning princess, sweetheart), and sings over her a beautiful love song. Of course, she longs to be loved, and she begins to believe him. It begins to change her.

She grows in seeing herself as a beloved woman. Her countenance brightens; her eyes come alive. Though she is not sure what her future will be, she's not concerned. She knows she is not trapped any longer in despair and in her life of unworthiness. Receiving love into her innermost being has catapulted her into a new life.

Our growing into Jesus' love and into our belovedness has the same impact on our lives, too.

* * * * *

In Victor Hugo's great story, *Les Misérables*, the hero Jean Valjean rescues Fantine from arrest and imprisonment. She was fired from her job at Valjean's factory. With no income, she is forced to sell her hair, then her teeth, and then her body (i.e., sex) to gain money to support her daughter Cosette. Fantine is sick and is dying, but Jean Valjean picks her up in his arms and carries her into his own house. She asks, "Why are you doing this?" And offers him her body as payment. He tells her he will send for and take care of Cosette. She says, "Don't you realize I am nothing more than a prostitute?" Jean Valjean says, "Not in God's eyes. You have always been God's child. You are still His child, whom He adores."

When we can hear those same words that Jesus speaks over us, and grow into those words as true for us, we are changed.

* * * * *

Disney's animated movie *Beauty and the Beast* continues to be voted the number one animated movie of all time.

It's the only animated movie ever nominated for a Best Picture Oscar.

Beauty and the Beast is the story of a normal guy, not a horrible guy. He's young, self-centered, and makes a few bad choices, and before he knows it, he's become a beast. He's stuck in his beastliness; He cannot change himself on his own. It's going to take something or someone outside of himself to save him/rescue him.

Along comes Belle, which means "the beautiful one." She enters his world; help comes from the outside. Long story short, in loving him, she rescues him. She doesn't see the beast he is; she sees his good heart...she sees the true him. And her love changes him into his true self.

But evil still lurks and doesn't want this change; so, evil attacks. All evil wants is for its own; evil tries to destroy what is not its own. There's a real battle, and evil loses. Not only does love win, but evil is forever defeated. And, a forever love, for which we all long, is found.

The reason this story feels so familiar is because it's the story of God's rescue of us. It's our story!

We don't mean to be hurtful, but as we live the self-life, we make some bad choices, and so, we all grow into some manner of a beast. We cannot break free from, or change from, our beastliness on our own. We must have something or someone from outside of us to come and rescue us.

So, "the Beautiful One" enters our world…the Belle is named Jesus, which means "the One Who Saves." In His love for us, he dies to remove our beastliness (which the Bible calls sin). Through and in His love, and in our receiving His love, we are made right; we become our true selves. But evil is present and constantly attacks to kill, steal, and destroy any knowledge of Jesus' love and any growing into our belovedness in Jesus. But because of Jesus' death on the cross, evil is defeated. With Jesus' resurrection, evil is defeated forever. Jesus' love wins, and a true, forever love, which we long for, can be ours. If we accept and embrace Jesus' love and grow into knowing our belovedness, we can live as "the disciple whom Jesus loves" for the rest of our days on earth, and then forever more.

CHAPTER 15

"There is tremendous relief in knowing that Jesus's love for me is utterly realistic, based at every point on prior knowledge of the worst about me, so that no discovery now can disillusion Him about me, in the way I am so often disillusioned about myself, and quench His determination to bless me."[46]

—J. I. Packer

The splendor of a human heart that is fully surrendered to the unconditional love of Jesus gives God more pleasure than the Sistine Chapel or 1,000 butterflies in flight.[47]

—Brennan Manning

"I planted, Apollos watered,
but God was causing the growth."

—The Apostle Paul (1 Corinthians 3:6)

Understanding that any growing into Jesus' love for us is a gift from God, and is a work of the Holy Spirit within us, is there anything we can do to help our growth?

I have always enjoyed walking through a greenhouse, where plants, flowers, shrubs, and seedlings are nurtured to the stage where they are ready to make it on their own in the outside world.

In the greenhouse, you can adjust the temperature to the best degree; you water the new growth just the right amount; you prepare the best soil for the plant to grow; and you fertilize perfectly. However, it is still God who grows the plant. You give the plant the very best chance to grow. You helped, of course, but it is God who grows the plant.

We can greenhouse our hearts to give ourselves the best chance for God to grow our knowing ourselves as "the disciple whom Jesus loves."

Remember, plants don't grow overnight. I know we no longer have to wait for photos to be developed. I know that Amazon often delivers the same day we place the order. I know that if we have to wait on hold on the phone or wait in a line to order food or to check out, we get irritated. But we cannot rush our growing into Jesus' love.

What then is the equivalent of setting the temperature, watering, soil, and fertilizer to greenhouse our hearts?

- Keep looking at the Cross because that's where you see Jesus' love best expressed for you. For the joy set before Jesus, He endured the cross... (Hebrews 12:2). What is "the joy" set before Him? Jesus' joy is our rescue completed, the barrier removed, so His love can be poured out on us and in us.
- Keep taking the Eucharist, the Sacrament of Communion, because you'll take into yourself Jesus' body broken and His blood shed out of His love for you. It is not only a continual reminder of Jesus' love for you, but also of receiving or taking His love into your innermost being.
- Be aware and name whatever it is that seems to be a blockage to internalizing Jesus' love for you, whatever keeps you from surrendering to His love for you. Naming it will begin to disarm it, and give the Holy Spirit a chance to heal it and remove it.
- As you live through difficult times, tribulation, and suffering, trust that God is using that time to possibly prune you (John 15:2), or discipline you (Hebrews 12:6), or, as St John of the Cross suggests: to purge from you any vain affections.[48] Remember that Jesus never abandons you, always living true to His promise: *I will be*

with you, every moment of every day (Matthew 28:20). Remember that Jesus *splochnas* you. He is entering in and bearing your pain with you. Remember that nothing in all creation can separate you from the love of God for you that is ours in Jesus (Romans 8:38-39). Remember that the people who have the deepest knowing of their belovedness in Jesus say that their tribulation (*lipsis*) grew them into Jesus' love more than anything else. I am one who makes that statement.

- Let God's beautiful creation, all with His imprint, speak to you, His very image-bearer, of His love.

It has been interesting to me when I speak to other followers of Jesus about growing into Jesus' love and of knowing their belovedness in Jesus. Many will make me feel like I'm living in La-La Land, that I'm speaking of something that is unrealistic. I agree; it is alien to our traditional, cultural understanding of discipleship or of growing closer to Jesus.

If you are reading this book and are this far along, you must sense your soul's longing for truly growing into Jesus' love. I'd encourage you to follow your heart and the longing you sense, for growing into an identity of "the disciple whom Jesus loves" is very real.

This book has also suggested some exercises that would be part of greenhousing our hearts.

- Pray for Jesus and His Spirit to move inside of you…Page 7
- Write your own Beloved Charter…Pages 16-19
- Relax in God's love and let it seep into your being. Marinate your heart in Jesus' love for you…Page 34
- Memorize Ephesians 3:14-19 (or rather "Hide God's Word in your heart…" Psalm 119:11) and pray it every day for your birthday month. Page 50
- Become more aware of shame in your life and call it out. Page 66
- Pray The Welcoming Prayer regularly. Page 106
- And finally, practice gratitude. Thank God for everything you can think of…daily. Gratitude fosters love, both the receiving of love and the giving of love.

EPILOGUE

"...keep yourself in the love of God..."
—Jude, 1:21

"May the Lord direct your hearts to the love of God..."
—2 Thessalonians 3:5

I know you through and through – I know everything about you. I know what is in your heart. I know especially your need for love – how you are thirsting to be loved and cherished. But how often have you thirsted in vain, by seeking that love selfishly, striving to fill the emptiness inside you with passing pleasures. Do you thirst for love? "Come to me all you who thirst." (John 7:37) I will satisfy you and fill you. I love you more than you can imagine to the point of dying on a cross for you. I thirst for you. Yes, that is the only way to even begin to describe my love for you: I thirst for you.[49]
—Mother Teresa
(writing from the perspective of Jesus)

Is it too weird or outlandish to characterize our relationship with Jesus as a "love affair" and not as a religion or beliefs about God and life? Is it false teaching, or an exaggeration, to say that a main part of our discipleship should be growing into Jesus' love, which brings about the transformation of our hearts and solidifies our identity as Jesus' beloved, so that we can truly live loved?

It seems to me that we must not let discipleship be only gaining more knowledge and getting the doctrines right, along with gritting our teeth to grind out our obedience to Jesus with great determination. Living to please God will then gravitate to being only duty or compliance. We will want to make sure we're doing enough to get heaven or to earn God's favor.

But doctrines and rules for living don't captivate our hearts. Rather, knowing we're loved by Jesus makes our living simply responding to His Love. Being obedient to God, keeping His Commandments, is loving Jesus back. It is joy-full to honor Him, not an obligation. His commands are seen as gracious invitations to more life. Knowing you're loved, you just live loved. Knowing you are the disciple whom Jesus loves, no matter what, does not give you permission to go do whatever you want; rather, you desire to love Jesus right back by doing what you know pleases Him (i.e., keeping His commands). Our submission to Jesus and giving Him our allegiance does not decrease with our growing into Jesus' love; rather, it increases.

Reframing the question, "How am I to love Jesus?" with "How am I to let myself be loved by Jesus?" lifts receiving Jesus' love to being essential. That's a difficult thing for us humans. It makes us vulnerable and out of control. Surrendering to Jesus' love characterizes our conversion and our discipleship. Many cannot or will not surrender.

Knowing we are loved by Jesus with no catch does not compromise God's holiness; Jesus' love is a Holy Love. Being the disciple whom Jesus loves does not weaken our view of sin. Yes, we do know that God, in His love for us, is not disgusted with us, nor withdrawing from us, because we still sin. But this truth draws us more to Him: We are loved by Jesus, no matter what.

I so hope this written effort has in some way helped you along your particular journey into Jesus' love and in knowing yourself as the disciple whom Jesus loves. And, in that identity, life for you is becoming lighter and freer, more joy-filled, and more secure, as you live loved, receiving and then responding to Jesus' loving you!

That's been my prayer for all who read it.

Ty Saltzgiver

You can find more books by
Ty Saltzgiver at **SaltResources.com**.
To connect with Ty directly, he can be
reached at **tysaltzgiver@gmail.com**.

ENDNOTES

1. Tozer, A. W. *The Pursuit of God*. New York: Harper & Row, 1948. My summary of the theme presented in this book.
2. Dallas Willard, *The Divine Conspiracy: Rediscovering Our Hidden Life in God* (San Francisco: HarperSanFrancisco, 1998), 338.
3. Henri J. M. Nouwen, *The Life of the Beloved: Spiritual Living in a Secular World* (New York: Crossroad, 1992), 37.
4. Brennan Manning, *Abba's Child: The Cry of the Heart for Intimate Belonging* (Colorado Springs: NavPress, 2002).
5. Jonathan Edwards, "Evidence that True Religion, in Great Part Consists in the Affections," in *The Works of Jonathan Edwards: Volume 2: Religious Affections*, ed. John E. Smith (New Haven, CT: Yale University Press, 2009).

6. Brennan Manning, *The Ragamuffin Gospel: Good News for the Bedraggled, BeatUp, and BurntOut* (Sisters, OR: Multnomah Publishers, 2005).
7. Augustine of Hippo, *On Grace and Free Will*, trans. R. E. Wallis (London: Methuen, 1952), 17. Augustine of Hippo, *On the Predestination of the Saints*, trans. R. E. Wallis (London: Methuen, 1952), 5. Augustine repeatedly insists on this in both of these books.
8. Victor Hugo, *Les Misérables: Book IX.*
9. Elizabeth Gilbert, *Committed: A Skeptic Makes Peace with Marriage* (New York: Viking, 2010).
10. A combining form - "all."
11. John Eldredge, *Wild at Heart: Discovering the Secret of a Man's Soul* (Nashville, TN: Thomas Nelson, 2001).
12. Richard J. Foster, *Celebration of Discipline: The Path to Spiritual Growth* (San Francisco: HarperSan-Francisco, 1998).
13. Trevor Hudson, *Seeking God: Finding Another Kind of Life with St. Ignatius and Dallas Willard* (Colorado Springs, CO: NavPress, 2022) 66-67. I was first introduced to the Beloved Charter idea in this book.
14. Dallas Willard, *The Divine Conspiracy. Rediscovering Our Hidden Life in God* (San Francisco: Harper-SanFrancisco, 1998.

Dallas Willard, *Renovation of the Heart: Putting on the Character of Christ* (Colorado Springs, CO: NavPress, 2002).

Dallas Willard, *The Great Omission: Reclaiming Jesus's Essential Teachings on Discipleship* (San Francisco, CA: HarperSanFrancisco, 2006). This principle is woven across Dallas Willard's writings on spiritual formation and disciple-making, notably from these books.

15. Yogi Berra, *The Yogi Book: I Really Didn't Say Everything I Said!* (New York: Workman Publishing Company, 1998).
16. Brennan Manning, *Abba's Child: The Cry of the Heart for Intimate Belonging* (Colorado Springs: NavPress, 2002).
17. A. W. Tozer, *The Knowledge of the Holy: The Attributes of God, Their Meaning in the Christian Life* (New York: Harper & Row, 1961), 9.
18. St. John of the Cross, *The Dark Night of the Soul*, trans. E. Allison Peers (New York: Image Books, 1959).
19. Paul David Tripp, *Suffering: Gospel Hope When Life Doesn't Make Sense* (Wheaton, IL: Crossway, 2010).
20. The Hebrew word is *radaph* which means "relentlessly chase after."
21. Julian of Norwich, *Revelations of Divine Love*, trans. Grace Warrack (London: J. M. Dent, 1901).

22. Brennan Manning, *The Ragamuffin Gospel: Good News for the Bedraggled, BeatUp, and BurntOut* (Sisters, OR: Multnomah Publishers, 2005). He recounts a story from the slave community around New Orleans as their way of discerning genuine conversion. There were no doctrinal questions; instead, they would ask this question.
23. Brennan Manning, *The Ragamuffin Gospel: Good News for the Bedraggled, BeatUp, and BurntOut* (Sisters, OR: Multnomah Publishers, 2005).
24. Spoken verbally by Brennan Manning in a sermon for a Solitude Retreat that I attended.
25. Brennan Manning, *The Ragamuffin Gospel: Good News for the Bedraggled, BeatUp, and BurntOut* (Sisters, OR: Multnomah Publishers, 2005). As Brennan Manning draws from Blaise Pascal (Penses) reminds us
26. Brennan Manning, *Souvenirs of Solitude: Finding Rest in Abba's Embrace* (Colorado Springs, CO: NavPress, 2009).
27. In John 17:3, the English word "eternal" (Greek word *aionis*), means more than everlasting (that's a different Greek word). *Aionis* means deep, rich, lasting life - a quality of life, thus the translation. I am also substituting *ginosko* for "know."
28. Timothy J. Keller, *Walking with God through Pain and Suffering* (New York: Dutton, 2013).

29. Thomas Keating, *Open Mind, Open Heart: The Contemplative Dimension of the Gospel* (New York: Continuum, 1986), 76.
30. Viktor E. Frankl, *Man's Search for Meaning* (Boston: Beacon Press, 1959).
31. Deuteronomy 22:22; Leviticus 20:10.
32. Two gentlemen who attended Eugene Peterson's Memorial Service said the highlight was Lief Peterson's eulogy. He said that his dad only had one sermon and that he spoke it over Lief every night when he thought his son was asleep. But some nights he was still awake and heard his dad.
33. Tests show that green is the easiest color on the human eye. This is what led to schools exchanging their blackboards for green ones.
34. C. S. Lewis, *The Screwtape Letters* (New York: HarperCollins, 2001), 98–102.
35. G. K. Chesterton, *Orthodoxy* (London: John Lane, 1908). Chesterton describes Christianity as a romance, as a love worth giving one's life to…that it is not a theory, but a thing like a love affair.
36. A. W. Tozer, *The Knowledge of the Holy: The Attributes of God, Their Meaning in the Christian Life* (New York: Harper & Row, 1961). Tozer observed that while many Christians readily confess belief in Jesus, far fewer are inwardly convinced of God's love for them.

37. Charles Wesley, *The Journals of Charles Wesley: Volume 2, 1738–1742*, ed. Kenneth G. C. Newport (Oxford: Clarendon Press, 1990).
38. I first heard God's commandments as "gracious invitations to more life" from Dale Bruner's teaching.
39. *Splochna* in the Gospels: Matthew 9:36, 14:14, 15:32, 18:27, 20:34; Mark 6:34, 8:2, 9:22 10:21; Luke 7:13, 10:33, 15:20.
40. St. John of the Cross, *The Living Flame of Love*, trans. E. Allison Peers (London: J. M. Dent, 1959). This idea comes from St. John of the Cross' Living Flame of Love, especially Stanza 1 (and his commentary on that stanza) where John describes God entering the soul as an all-consuming Lover.
41. G. K. Chesterton, *What's Wrong with the World* (London: Methuen & Co., 1910), Part I, Chapter IV.
42. François Fénelon, *Let Go: To Get Peace and Real Joy* (Springdale, PA: Whitaker House, 1973). Winn Collier paraphrases Francis Fenelon in Let Go: To Get Peace and Real Joy.
43. Thomas Keating, *Open Mind, Open Heart: The Contemplative Dimension of the Gospel* (New York: Continuum, 1986).
44. Reynolds Price, *A Palpable God: Thirty Stories Translated from the Bible with an Essay on the Origins and Life of Narrative* (New York: Atheneum, 1978).

45. Frederick Buechner, *The Magnificent Defeat* (New York: Seabury Press, 1966). My paraphrase.
46. J. I. Packer, *Knowing God* (Downers Grove, IL: InterVarsity Press, 1973), Chapter 19, "Sons of God," 258.
47. Brennan Manning, *Abba's Child: The Cry of the Heart for Intimate Belonging* (Colorado Springs: NavPress, 2002). My adaptation into one sentence from several sentences in the book.
48. St. John of the Cross, *The Dark Night of the Soul*, trans. E. Allison Peers (New York: Image Books, 1959).
49. Mother Teresa, *Come Be My Light: The Private Writings of the Saint of Calcutta*, edited by Brian Kolodiejchuk (New York: Doubleday, 2007). My collection of sentences from Mother Teresa's private spirituality and letters on her meditations on Jesus' words from the cross, "I thirst" (John 19:28).

www.ingramcontent.com/pod-product-compliance
Lightning Source LLC
LaVergne TN
LVHW010621100826
845148LV00014B/3066

* 9 7 8 1 6 3 2 9 6 9 7 9 8 *